# SACRED
# **CALL**
# IN
# SECULAR
# PLACES

...You were brought to the Kingdom for such a time as this!

## BARRINGTON F. GOLDSON

Copyright © 2011 by Barrington F. Goldson

*Sacred Call In Secular Places*
by Barrington F. Goldson

Printed in the United States of America

ISBN 9781609570354

All rights reserved solely by the author. The author guarantees all contents are original and do not infringe upon the legal rights of any other person or work. No part of this book may be reproduced in any form without the permission of the author. The views expressed in this book are not necessarily those of the publisher.

Unless otherwise indicated, Bible quotations are taken from The Holy Bible, King James Version (KJV).

www.xulonpress.com

Robert,

Rich family and friends are the top — few enjoy! Mary & you always be blessed by family & friends

[signature]
5/8/11

# SACRED CALL IN SECULAR PLACES

...You were brought to the Kingdom for such a time as this!

## BARRINGTON F. GOLDSON

Editorial Team
**Felicia Barracks**
**Krystal Goldson**
**Wayne Tulloch**
**Kim Williams**

Special thanks
To my editorial team
who worked tirelessly to help me publish this book.
Their contribution is invaluable and
forever appreciated.

Dedicated
To my wife **Jo-Ann** and children
**Lennox** and **Krystal**; who are the center of my life
…and the **Calvary Tabernacle family**; who is the center of
Apostolic activity in
Nassau County, New York.

Cover Design: **Robert Stewart**
Many thanks
for designing the cover for this book.
His contribution to this project is invaluable and
forever appreciated.

# Table of Contents

## Chapters

*Prologue* ..................................................................... xv

**1 Trauma** ................................................................. 19
- Childhood Trauma ............................................. 21
- Lifestyle Trauma ................................................ 24
- Cultural Trauma ................................................ 25
- Socioeconomic Trauma ..................................... 27
- Emotional Trauma ............................................. 29
- Iconic Traumatic Occurrences .......................... 34

**2 Training** ................................................................ 43
- Parental / Caregiver Training ........................... 43
- Secular Training ................................................. 58
- Priestly Training ................................................ 74
- God's Training ................................................... 79
- Learning To Wait On Your Sacred Call .......... 81
- Execution Of Call .............................................. 83

**3 Triumph** ............................................................... 87
- Tools of Triumph .............................................. 87
- Taste of Triumph .............................................. 94

*References* ................................................................ 103

# Prologue

While I was growing up, as early as six years old, I recognized the hierarchal structure in our home. My father was the Chief Executive Officer and provider. As a hard worker, his focus was to provide for the family, so he spent many hours at his regular job and fishing business in Jamaica. My mother was the Chief Operating Officer and counselor. As a stay-at-home mother she was responsible for the overall functions at home. An excellent organizer and delegator who had her staff of five, the children. We took charge of anything we could possibly manage, while she measured the results at intervals to ensure that the rules were followed. Homework and chores had to be done before playtime, and when it was time for dinner, we all had to be present at the table.

As time went on the familial company crashed and Mom had to take a new role. During this time, we had to "make do" with what Mom could provide. The five of us, three boys and two girls were each other's keeper and we had to protect and share with each other. Interestingly, we never received equal increments of money, clothes or even food…instead we were recipients according to our age. Being the middle child out of the three boys I was the recipient of what seemed to be the brunt of the chores and the short end of the bargains. They ranged from clothes that passed from my older brother to recycled books and toys, but it was "all good" because I knew Mom could not afford the luxury of new ones. In time I learned to appreciate whatever came my way, because it was always better to have, than not to have.

I saw the hand of God move in my life when He stepped in as a Father and used the Salvation Army as a provider to assist us during this transitional period of my life. That was my first encounter with God's ability as a provider, and I started learning from that very moment that I could trust God to always provide. This would later help me in my sacred call and gave me much confidence as I trafficked in secular places.

As a family we had happy times and there was a sense of appreciation and belonging. I thrived on promises and hoped to see a better day. I learned the ideas of self-motivation, self-reliance, determination, morality and self-denial. And, I believe that we understood honesty and loyalty, and fully embraced the value of family and community. We were taught especially how to relate to the public and keep our heads high; and we never wore our stripes on our shoulders. We could sit with kings and still remember our common ground, and most of all we knew that where we were today did not dictate where we were going and what we would become. My mother, who loved to sew, always said, "We have to stay on crooked and cut straight" which means, to stay on the current path, and create your way out of it.

My transition into elementary school was met with great fear. I was introverted and reserved because I had a lisp. I was afraid of ridicule when it was time for oral reading or spelling and math bees. What a trauma that was for me as a child! I found expression, however, in what I did not know at that age was my sacred call. While I would not speak in school, I preached in my "sanctuary" to my outdoor congregation of trees and rocks during my playtime.

I approached high school with great anticipation: determined to put my elementary fears behind me; building on the confidence of receiving a scholarship and being accepted to the high school of my choice.

During my high school years it became more evident that my childhood call was not a fantasy. As a result I developed a mindset that was different from my family and friends. I wanted to be priestly while they wanted to party! At times the call was powerful but still felt very inconvenient. I wanted to be like everybody else but I knew I was different. I thrust my energy into the debate team I joined, excelling in school, and enjoying the high school experience.

After High School I met Jo-Ann, who later became my beautiful bride and wife. We plunged our minds into the books and our spirits into the things of God. Under the pastoral teaching and mentoring of Pastor Samuel Stewart, the pastor of a powerful and influential church, we began to understand quite clearly what John meant when he said, "Beloved, I wish above all things that thou mayest prosper and be in health, even as thy soul prospereth" (3 Jhn. 1:1-2). We understood the thought that wisdom builds but knowledge establishes and so we learned to create a balance with the sacred and secular and studied to show ourselves approved unto God. We were champions in Bible Quizzing tournaments, pacemakers creating, developing, transforming and establishing young minds towards excellence.

A short while later we migrated to New York. The call and mandate from the Lord was made plainer and my spirit was overwhelmed with the enormity of the call. Simultaneously, the need to fulfill my sacred call and human desires started to unsettle the equilibrium Jo-Ann and I had mastered. Oh the emotional trauma!

I started out, juggling local jobs in the city and then went on the fast track to become Assistant Vice-President of a prominent bank in New York. Still, that was not my final stop. The call of the Lord was to become a Pastor; to provide spiritual guidance to others and to minister to their spiritual and related needs. I felt compelled to listen to the inner appeal. This challenge could not be taken lightly. This challenge was of such that some of my friends could not comprehend it. My education helped me to identify with the cultural diversity but the spiritual propensity that delivered the true necessities was totally dependent on God. It was during this time that the pastoral mentoring of Pastor Lincoln Graham, Sr. the pastor of a fast- growing Church was invaluable. Here, God blessed us with two children, Lennox and Krystal. I soon realized that God at times does not call a man only, but calls a family. My family has been an example of a sacred family call. Together we have embraced this call and each of us, in our unique way, has made a significant and notable contribution to the kingdom of God.

My hunger and thirst after righteousness led me to evaluate the lifestyle and principles of biblical characters and their relevance in our day. Moses stood out to me in particular because his speech impediment was similar to mine.

Moses was a child born into slavery during the time when the pharaohs of Egypt were reaping wealth from the labor of enslaved Israelites. God who promised them a messiah heard their cries of cruelty. The news brought great fear among the hierarchal authority of the pharaohs and a decision was made to annihilate every child born to the slaves in order to abort the promise of a messiah. Into this atmosphere came Moses; placed by his mom in an ark upon the river that was to be the deathbed of all Israelite male babies. What was meant to be his demise led him to his destiny. Where others were slain he was salvaged. This childhood trauma led him into his sacred call as the deliverer of God's people.

**Sacred Call in Secular Places** is prepared to meet you at whatever point you are in your sacred journey today. Its intent is to create a bridge of transition towards the earnest expectations that the Lord has for you. God speed as we journey together to the other side because …you were brought to the Kingdom for such a time as this!

# 1 Trauma

*"And the woman conceived, and bare a son: and when she saw him that he was a goodly child, she hid him three months".*
*Exodus 2:2*

Everyone at some point in their life has been through some form of trauma, nobody is exempt. We are told that traumas which may have more lasting effects on adults are those experienced during the childhood years.

Some children experienced physical abuse during their formative years. This type of abuse may leave permanent scars, as many times the children are beaten with objects which often show signs of their physical injury.

Children may also experience emotional abuse. In this case the child may be deprived of love, affection and or acceptance within the family. These children may experience the emotional scars of the criticism, ridicule and verbal abuse they received on a regular basis. There is an old saying that goes like this, "sticks and stones may break my bones but words will never hurt me" (pp.12 Saisan, Jaffe-Gill, & Segal 2009). "This old saying could not be farther from the truth. Emotional child abuse may seem invisible. However, because emotional child abuse involves behavior that interferes with a child's mental health or social development, the effects can be extremely damaging and may even leave deeper lifelong psychological scars than physical abuse" (pp.12 Saisan, Jaffe-Gill, & Segal 2009).

Some children may experience sexual abuse. Children exposed to this type of situation are often left feeling confused, unclean and guilty.

Even when the abuse is only observed, the emotional effects are obvious among children who have seen their parents inflict both physical and emotional pain upon each other. This indirect experience may cause children to have difficulty coping with themselves.

Another form of abuse that a child may receive is in the form of neglect. Neglect takes place when there is a failure to provide for the shelter, safety, supervision and nutritional needs of the child. This type of abuse can prove to be quite traumatic for a child.

It is clear that abuse in any form can negatively impact a child's current and future behavior. It is incumbent upon every parent and caregiver to ensure that they take the necessary precautions not to abuse their children in any way and to protect their children from any form of abuse by a third party.

Overall any kind of abuse can be detrimental toward the smooth transition from childhood to adulthood. Some people have had a wonderful childhood experience, but later on in their lives they encounter challenges and unfortunate circumstances that give rise to traumatic experiences.

## ♦ Childhood Trauma

Whenever someone is called by God and is assigned to do great things, we observe that they experience extensive traumatic occurrences in the early stages of their lives. The intent is to distract, pervert and sway them from the intended course. The devil knows that if these people ever get to the point of focus where they discover their gifts, calling and purpose; they will gather the tenacity that is embedded deep within their spirit to execute their intended destiny. That person is going to create havoc in the devil's kingdom. The trauma that the devil uses was not created by him, he is only the executioner. Trauma was added for the punishment of sin, it was a part of the curse that Adam and Eve received from their guilty verdict.

The scripture says that God shall greatly multiply the woman's sorrow and her conception; and in sorrow she shall bring forth children (Gen. 3:16). Every maternal ward has the scar of child bearing; it is a witness to the accomplishment of the word of the Lord. Every child is born in sin and shaped in iniquity. Therefore our first appearance into the world is through the curse of sin. That is to say, at birth every child enters the world through a physical traumatic scenario; no one is exempt.

Upon reviewing biblical patterns it is apparent that God would always name things and testify of them before they came into being. We find that He will call simple men princes that are presently peasants, and that which is least he will call great. Whether it pertains to a group of people, an individual or an event, His words precede the evidence of the actual and transform impotence into prominence.

The devil and his team do not have prior knowledge of what God will do next, so they are attentive listeners for the spoken word. God always speaks audible so that they can hear because He knows that they are the catalyst of the reactions. In the same manner that God promised Jesus and testified of his purpose long before His arrival on the scene, and as He did with Moses and many of the prophets; similarly, Job's scenario was initialized with God expressing sentiments of his values and eventualities, and the devil heard, drew near to listen and challenge.

Likewise, a relative conversation of our destiny was spoken in the heavenly long before we were born and the demons heard it. They went ahead to construct terminal circumstances and lines of demarcation in an atmosphere conducive to death, damage and disease. They eagerly awaited our birth to ensure that we would not succeed.

The question here is, what is the reason that demons have such intense anger against us that they want to destroy the very cradle of our dependence long before we arrive? The answer is quite simple. Apart from the war in heaven and the banishment of the devil and his supporters to the earth, God did a new thing to redeem the earth, he created man in his image and likeness, ranked him a little lower than angels, crowned him with glory and placed him upon a paradise earth with dominion much to the devil's annoyance. The scripture states that in the beginning when God created man, he blessed them collectively, and declared unto them saying, be fruitful, and multiply, and replenish the earth, and subdue it: and have dominion... (Gen. 1:28). The devil heard this. The declaration was certified, sealed and signed, and applicable to every human being.

The declaration did not subscribe to weakness and impotence it did not foster drought nor indifference, instead it spoke to prosperity, power, soundness of mind and continuity; it was a collection of God's out-poured favor towards man. That declaration has become the contributing factor that attracts all adversarial attacks; hence there is always a set stage and a favorable atmosphere to foster our hurt, even from birth, that we should abort the rite of purpose.

As mentioned earlier the first traumatic experience that I vividly remember is having a lisp as a young boy. The lisp was so pronounced that it incapacitated or handicapped my entire perception and my social development. In addition, I was a sickly child; I visited the hospital so much that the entire hospital staff knew me by name. I thought that this impediment made me different from the other children and this caused extensive fear that greatly impacted my life. I became an introvert. I could not enter the school system at the appropriate age as everyone did, because of my fears and this trauma.

My mother sheltered me from my fears of the school and sent me to a neighborhood scholar to teach me the lessons taught in school until I was able to abate my fears. When I entered public school, it was as if I went there as a formality or procedure. None of my teachers expected me to excel, and of course I did not, at least, not at that time. I was assessed as being at the bottom ten percent of the class, and this was a very big class. I personally knew that this was not a reflection of my academic ability but no one else knew. The examinations at that level were predominantly oral. I could analyze and interpret the questions but I would not verbally relate or express myself. No one really knew the internal frustration that I was experiencing. This was a direct plot to abort my purpose to speak and declare with boldness "Thus saith the Lord."

While Eve accounts for the trauma that we arrive in, Adam on the other hand accounts for our inability to strive and the challenges we experience to achieve upward mobility. The ground was cursed for his sake and whenever it brought forth sustenance it would come through thorns and thistle i.e. hindrance and restrictions. His curse was so intense that it states implicitly that if a man does not work he should not eat (2 Thess. 3:10).

Though Jesus freed us from those curses, the devil kept a portrait and creates a physical resemblance in every facet of life. The foggy replication of the Adamic curse that the devil revises is so thick that mankind can hardly see themselves through it to success.

Whether it is cultural, socio-economical or family related hindrances; there are life-threatening situations strategically set to destroy us, even from our youth. Let us look in depth at these possible effects starting with cultural hindrances to upward mobility.

### ♦ Lifestyle Trauma

Lifestyle trauma in the form of culture is not unique to race or religion because culture rules in almost every facet of our lives, even though sometimes we are completely unaware of this. Most people tend to define culture as music, language, dance and religion while others say that culture is the way of life of a people. However, some scholars, identified culture as *what we do, think and feel* (Centre for Intercultural Learning). Culture is further defined as what is taught, learned, shared and passed down from one generation to the next, with the hope that it will survive for a very long time. Culture is vital because it enables the members within a given society to function with each other without the need to consult the meaning of every aspect of life. It is significant because as we work with others it both enables us and impedes us in our ability to understand and work effectively together (Centre for Intercultural Learning).

However, in many cultures the hierarchal ladder of success has never been climbed by ordinary people with ease and contentment. It has rarely been climbed with prepared fortification or individual spontaneous effort. You may not subscribe to this philosophy; however, it is almost impossible to refute when examined. It is clear that a premise has been distorted when you evaluate the percentage of people of ordinary means who do not succeed. There is interference in this arena since success was a part of the declaration.

## ♦ Cultural Trauma

Cultural hindrances can be a high point for setbacks for many people. What may be considered to be the norm in one country may very well be a crime in another. So for persons migrating to other countries where norms are different they may find themselves paying the penalty for what was not a crime in their country of origin. That's the power of culture! Its pressure persuades you to conform to the norms of the society in which you live. An example of this is the practice of Polygamy in parts of Africa, which in that culture is an acceptable norm. Africans migrating to the United States (US) may have to leave Polygamy behind as the law in the US prohibits such a practice (Polygamy in Africa from a young Africans' point of view, 2010).

The Caste system in India is a kind of cultural hindrance to upward mobility. The Caste system is a system used for social stratification and has some form of restrictions for its people. Although many societies could be described in this way, within the caste system, people are rigidly expected to marry and interact with people of the same social class. There are four major castes and the fifth one is considered to be the caste-less, often referred to as the untouchables. This system of caste is a perfect example that can be used to prevent upward mobility among the ambitious (The Caste System in Hinduism, 2010).

In the heart of Corporate America I experienced the silent yet savvy culture of the 1980's and 1990's. That culture was defined by the blue, black and grey suits worn by both men and women on Wall Street; a few blocks from where I worked at the time. During that period, if you wore a brown suit to an interview we knew that you were from out of town. Imagine the trauma you felt once you recognized that you were not acceptable. If you were fortunate to be hired in that suit, you quickly updated your wardrobe to ensure upward mobility. It was commonly mentioned that one origin of the IBM nickname "Big Blue" was a reference to the color of their suits.

A religious culture that is now common in the Caribbean is Rastafarianism. Most Rastafarians consider themselves to be vegetarians. They eat limited types of meat or no meat at all. This dietary practice they embrace is adopted from the dietary Laws of Leviticus and Deuteronomy in the Old Testament (Rastafari Religion, 2009). In the 1970s, their strict dietary practices and rigid attitude towards "forbidden foods" severely affect their nutrition, especially that of growing children. This was before we had all the protein alternatives that we can eat today. Their culture also requires them not to cut their hair, which they indicate is adopted from the Biblical Nazarite's vow. During the 1970s their children may have experienced difficulty learning (trauma) in school because of these cultural conditions: the absence of some basic nutritional essentials in their diet; and low self-esteem due to ridicule from other children regarding their hair locks. Again, this was before hair locks became fashionable.

### ♦ Socio-economic Trauma

Socio-economic conditions also have an impact on childhood upbringings. According to information taken from Wikipedia, the free on-line encyclopedia, "socio-economics is the study of the relationship between economic activity and social life". Having this working definition of the main idea one can now make a valid comparison between two main thoughts; economic activity and social life.

The more economic power or advantage one has, the better quality of life he or she may be able to enjoy and maintain. All families need economic stability to afford a good quality of life.

In any given society, the social and economic conditions of one's family greatly determine the quality of life to be enjoyed by its members. A family's social and economical status is structured on the family's ability to earn an income and provide sound parental guidance for the children in the family. Also, the ability to involve the family in community-based organizations usually helps to strengthen family ties. Such organizations could be the church, the school, the public library or other social organizations.

Most families classified with a high socio-economical status often enjoy success in preparing their children for entry into the public or private school system with little or no level of frustration (North Central Regional Educational Laboratory, 2009). Families who are fortunate to acquire and maintain a solid social and economical backbone will no doubt be able to have access to a wide range of resources to promote and support their children's development. They will be able to provide members of the family with high quality health care and educational materials, which will encourage good learning habits. Also, they will have easy access to information that will contribute to the families' wellbeing.

Families classified with a low socio-economic status in society tend to lack in the financial, social, and educational arenas, which distinguish them from families with a high socio-economic status. Poor families tend to have insufficient access to community-based resources that promote and support children's development and school-readiness. Parents may also have inadequate skills for such activities such as: reading to, and with their children; lack of information about health issues and nutrition for their children.

Having inadequate resources and limited access to available resources can negatively affect families' decisions regarding their young children's development and learning. As a result, children from families with low socio-economic status are at greater risk of entering the public school system unprepared when compared to their peers from families with a higher level of socio-economic status (North Central Regional Educational Laboratory, 2009). Hence it is clear that socio-economical impediment of an individual directly affects their state of living. A person's social wellbeing will always be affected by their economical affluence. The inability to afford basic necessities can have drastic repercussions on the most disciplined of families. This can give rise not only to present recession but can be a cause of future aggression. Food, shelter and clothing are at the core of basic needs hence; if within a family these basic needs cannot be afforded, members will ultimately be at a disadvantage with possible traumatic results.

♦ **Emotional Trauma**

Some children have experienced the trauma of pain associated with broken homes and subsequent single parent upbringing, pining after the missing parent and at times blaming one of the parents or themselves for the separation. They often bear emotional scars, hold grudges and as a result end up fostering bitterness and unforgiveness. Some may have been born to parents that are financially challenged who chose to satisfy household amenities over educational opportunities. Some because of their previous pampered lifestyle become bitter, so much so that they become mean-spirited with selfish pride and find it difficult to go forward and integrate with society.

Some have been born to abusers, some under slavery, others unwanted and given up for adoption. Many are born in war-prone areas and have become a product of their environment. Good people, God's people, arriving into the world under unpleasant circumstances. Some were verbally and physically abused and some incarcerated.

Some kids were so devastatingly disturbed in the environment that they arrived in that they became manic-depressive, numb to any possible help. Some became prisoners of their situation and needed professional psychiatric treatment. Many died under their circumstances; others became disabled, crippled and scarred. The children born to these horrible situations paid an extremely high price for their uncaused predicament and are prone to become emotionally withdrawn, angry and gang-involved. Some may display anxiety, fear, and acute traumatic stress. In the paragraphs and chapters following we will revisit some of these traumatic occurrences for effect but first, let us travel upstream along this tangent and see what we find.

The matrix of traumatic sources that people have arrived to are enumerable, yet none of these complicated experiences are limited to race, sex, culture or even geographical origin. Governments upon identifying the magnitude of these profuse sores have put into place band-aid solutions. Programs such as welfare assistance, government clinics, soup kitchens, free lunches, adoptions, scholarships, sports and shelters were designed to divert lack and reduce the inevitable, resulting crime in society, yet indicators show that the wounds are leaking profusely.

In the same breath, however, if we search throughout history many of the great names and faces that are on plaques in libraries across the country, many statesmen and women, many dignitaries and elites have all had similar challenges. They can relate to the system of hardship and socio-economic failures. Many will tell you that they choose to live through blood, sweat and tears and live they did to the best. In spite of the environment, in spite of their circumstances, God brought them through. Some, whose parents did not send them to college, they marginally passed the eighth grade level but still they survived. They came into their atmosphere with a tenacity and resilience in their spirit that told them that the environment must not determine the outcome of their lives. Some lived among thieves and have never stolen. Others lived among prostitutes and did not sell their bodies. Many lived among drug dealers and never sold drugs. There must be a secret to their success. Their method through their madness can serve as a manual for the less fortunate. Let's explore this!

There is nothing new under the sun and with every temptation there is an escape route provided. No philosopher can take total credit in any academia, not even the writers of The Bible can claim that they, through their experiences had authored the script of success. The very writers said that the Holy Spirit moved upon them, meaning that God inhabited them and they wrote the scriptural manual.

It is reasonable then to say that the men and women who have triumphed in this life did tap into the spiritual declaration concerning their circumstances and found their purpose and thus prevailed. Whether by divine or default, whether it was taught or caught: no one can make it through without God, whether saved or unsaved. The ones that made it are the ones who saw their stumbling blocks as stepping-stones to get them higher. They are the ones that learned from observation instead of experience. They chose faith instead of fear and sacrificed the temporary pleasures for the future luxuries through study, investment and discipline. They are the ones who conceived the thought of living to see a better day. They are the ones that sought help, looked diligently for the escape opportunity and enthusiastically embraced the hope that fell through the cracks.

For those who have not read the heavenly script in the form of The Bible, the manual was not only written there; the great architect wrote it upon the face of nature. If you look up at the sky you will see that sometimes it is overcast and dark, you will hear fearful thunders and see frightening lightening and rainfalls. Sometimes it transforms into storms and hurricanes creating havoc: but after the storm the radiant sun will always rise again in its glory and splendor through shimmering white clouds.

God was there at the beginning and He is there at the end. He is the Author and Finisher and He rules in the affairs of men. For example, if you consider the earth: there are hills and there are valleys; rivers and seas; flowers that bloom; and birds that sing. Yet there are volcanoes, earthquakes and tsunamis, but that does not take away from the beauty that we experience here. Hence the heavens declare the glory of God and the firmament shows his handy works. Everything was designed to help us see that tough times do not last; tough people do.

Portraits of scriptural lessons are embedded throughout nature for our good. Looking back, I can appreciate some specific inconveniences of childhood trauma knowing that it brought me to a point of early maturity. It brought me to the point of where the choice was either do or die, break or bend. A point where the "blame game" and 'status quo' were not enough. A point where excuses were inexcusable and the horns of the bull were the steering wheel to deliverance and I had to hold it for control. A point at which my mother would have said, "stay on crooked and cut straight."

Of course, we were powerless over the childhood trauma that is a part of our calling. Knowing this, we can take the guilt off ourselves because we were not contributors nor were we willing participants. We must learn to let it go.

We can choose to become stagnant, make hardships our master and spend valuable time saturating ourselves with the legacy of childhood trauma and become drunk with that spirit thereof. We can embrace it and allow the memories to shape our future, or we can talk about it until it loses its savor. We can choose to use it as a measuring stick for our shortcomings, insecurities and missed opportunities or we could take the high road and flip the script. We could be thankful for the opportunity afforded us that we were not the ones that fell through the cracks and while we mourn the loss of many others, we could become role models for many to come. We could liken ourselves in our experiences as unto diamonds that are made under pressure and gold that is purified by heat, we can be likened unto myrrh that has to be crushed to emit the sweet smelling savor or the diversity of mixture that creates the anointing oil.

This, however, is not an endorsement for childhood abuse; for parents are to cover their children's wellbeing by all legitimate means. Instead it is my advice to you: if you are at an age that you can recognize and distinguish between good and evil; if you are at an age where you can be held accountable; if you are at the age where you realize that you deserve better; then you are at the age to accept realities, cry out for help and make the very best of a traumatic situation because everyone is subject to a taste of the devil's medicine.

Though we spent much time in this chapter delving into the traumatic occurrences that affect the growth and upward mobility of children of all ages, we have by no means exhausted the many contexts of these traumas. Neither is this book limited to only those that occur in childhood. Adults also face trauma from time to time and the diversified contexts are inexhaustible. While children look towards caregivers and the environment to receive change in their experiences, adults must look directly to training. Most times the scars that maim adults can be corrected therapeutically or through discipline and training.

To prove that, here is a list of Biblical testimonies and people who have been there and done that, real people that we know, love, admire or can relate to; prominent figures that have had their share of childhood trauma, but in spite of it all, they triumphed into great leaders, role models and career practitioners. We will begin with Jesus, our Lord and Savior, and follow with Moses, one of the greatest leaders of all time. Also, following these are the more current figures of Oprah right through to our current President Obama.

## ♦ Iconic Traumatic Occurrences

### *Jesus*

I love to read the book of Matthew and in particular, the genealogy of Jesus Christ. One would have thought that his ancestral tree would have been of impeccable standing because He is God, yet there was great instability. An ancestral great…, great grandmother was a whore, and if that is not bad enough, there are men in his lineage whose hands were so deep into blood that they were not worthy to build the house of the Lord. The men ranged from idolaters and adulterers to those who were involved in variable acts of the sinful sort.

His entrance into the world was no different either because it can be deduced that his mother was accused of being guilty of an out of wedlock teenage pregnancy. Let us think this story through thoroughly. Although it was prophesied that a virgin should conceive and bring forth the messiah, it is obvious that the Jews expected that a high societal family with leadership background would have this child. For by what viable means would poor Mary and Joseph instill the qualities in their child to become a world leader? Could this be why they did not find room among families and in the inn, even though they were from the same city?

The Jews are a highly religious set of people with the expectation that God would provide the solution to their problems. Now, here is a woman carrying Him in pregnancy, why was there no red carpet rolled out? There must have been a stigma concerning His virgin birth why his families did not welcome them into their homes even though Mary was great with child. The place they went to pay taxes was in fact, Bethlehem, which is the city of David. Joseph was of the house and lineage of David (Luke 2:4). But He was born among animals in a stable.

Not long afterwards his parents had to flee like refugees, taking asylum in another country because Herod was killing all the male, two years old and under, in order to get to Jesus. Even his transition into ministry was not a smooth one. He was hated by all religious leaders who tried to kill him with every chance they got, and eventually they did. Some would say that He could deal with it for He is the God man and I totally agree. But what do you say of his parents who were very young and had to deal with the entire emotional trauma and are as human as you and I? Trauma does not only affect non-Christian people. It bites into the greatest of Christians.

**Moses**

Moses was a child born to slaves in Egypt and much like the time and birth of Jesus, the Pharaohs, like Herod, were killing babies. The Pharaohs ordered that all the male children should be cast into the river. Moses' fate would have been no different from his peers, only he was hid in an ark.

The thought that captures my attention most concerning Moses is the fact that when God sent him in the latter days to go and speak to Pharaoh, he complained of a speech impediment. Could this mean that it was a direct result of him being locked up in the ark during his cognitive developmental period? Here is a three-month old infant in a dark box built with pitch, bulrushes and slime floating to nowhere upon a river engulfed with the stench of dead bodies, at the mercy of every imaginable type of carnivorous river creature and blood sucking insect. He never had people speaking around him; therefore he never heard nor learned to distinguish sounds in order to develop his phonetic skills at the time and age required. He was in a deep dark, solitary doom. Yet he came out to be one of the most prominent leaders in the Bible.

## *Oprah Winfrey*

Oprah Winfrey was born in Kosciusko, Mississippi, where she was raised by her grandmother, on a farm. During her early childhood, an indication of her future successful career was noticed by those around her. By the age of three, Oprah was learning to read aloud, recite and perform. Between the ages of six and thirteen she was sent to live with her mother in Milwaukee. While at her mother's home she suffered various forms of abuse and molestation. This attack on Oprah's young life was almost unbearable for her and she was left with no option but to run away. She was later sent to a juvenile detention home at the age of thirteen, only to be denied admission because all the beds were filled. As a last resort, she was sent to Nashville to live with her father Vernon Winfrey.

Vernon Winfrey was a strict disciplinarian who saw to it that his daughter met a midnight curfew, and ensured that she read a book and wrote a book report each week. "As strict as he was," says Oprah, "he had some concerns about me making the best of my life, and would not accept anything less than what he thought was my best" (American Academy of Achievement, 2009).

How did she survive such devastation at a young age and where did she gather the strength to carry on? I believe she woke up many nights scared to death from the intrusion of prevailing nightmares, and sobbed herself to sleep on tear-soaked pillows. I believe she cringed at the thoughts whenever they invaded her mind as she struggled to maintain her bearing and disposition.

She must have had insensitive friends to whom she could not mention her traumatic experience and hoped that they never caught wind of it for fear of further abuse. The pains did not stop there, I believe that as she grew the toughest battle was to learn forgiveness, shed the hurts and pains and look towards a brighter day.

## Maya Angelou

Maya Angelou, born Marguerite Annie Johnson in St. Louis, Missouri. Her parents divorced when she was only three and she was sent with her brother, Bailey, to live with their grandmother in the small town of Stamps, in Arkansas. While living in Stamps, Maya experienced racial discrimination, which then was the legally enforced way of life in the American South.

Despite the harsh realities of the day Maya looked beyond her circumstances and forged ahead by absorbing the deep religious faith and old-fashioned courtesy of traditional African American life. This decision gave her hope that one day things would be better. She credited her grandmother and her extended family for instilling in her good values that helped to formulate her adult life and career. She enjoyed a close relationship with her brother, who gave her the nickname Maya when they were very young (America Academy of Achievement, 2009).

When Maya was just seven years old she was raped by her mother's boyfriend. She confided in her beloved brother and told him of the incident. In little time the brother sought justice for her and reported the matter to her uncle who killed the molester. Maya was so ashamed and sad because she thought that because she spoke of her abuse the molester was killed. As a result of the incident she refused to speak for years. By age thirteen Maya and her brother rejoined her mother. At this time she found the courage to speak again. At this point in her life she saw her dream of being a poet, dancer and singer coming to reality. But, not too long after the thought lingered of a promising future with her new found love of her career, she became pregnant and dropped out of school.

Maya had a difficult life after the birth of her son. She had to do many odd jobs just to survive as a single mother. One thing was certain for Maya; she would not give up on her career goals (American Academy of Achievement, 2009).

You may be thinking, how more traumatic can it get and what did we all do to deserve all this, why are we in a war that we have not started, why do good people have such bad experiences and why is the devil so mad at us? Believe it or not, we are in a war...a war for the soul.

## Whoopi Goldberg

Whoopi Goldberg was born Caryn Johnson in New York City and is also considered a prominent figure, that people love.

Whoopi's mother was a nurse and teacher who struggled to take care of her and her brother. Her mother was left with no choice of raising them all by herself after her preacher father left the family. The single mother and her two children had to resort to living in a public housing project in Manhattan.

Although life was tough for the family Whoopi found some talent within her, and was never afraid to express her talent. Drawn to the theater from an early age, she made her performing debut at age eight with the Helena Rubinstein Children's Theatre at the Hudson Guild. After dropping out of high school at fourteen, she lied about her age to find work as a summer camp counselor, and singing in the choruses of the Broadway shows Hair, Jesus Christ Superstar and Pippin. Whoopi had some bad experiences with drug abuse in her early years but managed to survive the addiction. She later got married and gave birth to a daughter, Alexandrea (American Academy of Achievement, 2009).

All these iconic figures have tasted of trauma in some form or the other, from speech impediments similar to mine, single mother upbringing, molestation, teenage pregnancy and rape to name a few. Yet they came through with a drive and tenacity that only God could have instilled into their spirit – a call!

## James Earl Jones

James Earl Jones, a well known actor and writer was not without scar. He too was from a poor background and suffered tremendously during his early childhood years because of the separation of his parents, which took place before he was born. As a result of the separation he was sent to be raised by his grandparents. At the age of five his family moved north to a farm in rural Michigan, where he found the adaptation so traumatic that he developed a stutter. For many years he spoke a few words at a time. However, at school he communicated only in writing and began to express himself by writing poetry. Being poetic, he became a very good writer to the astonishment of his teacher, who at one point thought that the child who hardly ever spoke could not write so well (American Academy of Achievement, 2009).

Trauma never stops at damaging the socioeconomic structure and the environment that we all arrive in; it always moves to strike people who are endowed to become great orators and career practitioners, people whose names are going to be great, people with voices and a podium to effect positive change.

## Nelson Mandela

Nelson Mandela was a man that many people wished never existed, while others hoped that they had his courage and strength of character. Mandela's public image and status was born out of extreme hardship and perseverance. For the greater part of his productive adult life, he was imprisoned for his belief against apartheid. The experiences Mandela had, never deterred him from having his dream of working with the people of South Africa (Mandela Biography 2010).

### Sonia Sotomayor

Sonia Sotomayor had her fair share of socioeconomic hardships during childhood upbringing. She was raised in the Bronx housing projects, basically in poverty. Sonia was diagnosed with juvenile diabetes (type 1) when she was eight years old. Her father died when she was only nine years old, resulting in a single parent upbringing (Sotomayor Biography, 2010). Though raised against the backdrop of hardship, she never became a causality of her environment

### President Ronald Reagan

Ronald Reagan, the 40$^{th}$ President of the United States had his fair share of ups and down while climbing the ladder of his political career. Reagan never won the Republican presidential nomination on his first attempt. But his defeat never allowed him to go into a despondent mood. He used his disappointments to build his strength and moved ahead of adversities to acquire his deepest of dreams – the presidency of the United States of America (Ronald Reagan 2010).

### President Barack Obama

The 44$^{th}$ president of the United States of America, Barack Hussein Obama, born to a white American mother, Ann Dunham, and a black Kenyan father, Barack Obama, Sr., was no exception to childhood trauma. He too had his share of childhood misfortunes. His parents at the time of his birth were both young college students at the University of Hawaii. Barack's father received a scholarship to attend the University of Harvard which he accepted, leaving Barack and his mother behind.

His father later returned alone to Kenya, where he worked as a government economist. Barack's mother later remarried an Indonesian oil manager and moved Barack to that country at age six. Barack saw his father once at the age of ten, and spoke of exposure to poverty in Indonesia. Despite the hardship faced by his family during his early childhood years, his grandparents managed to send him to one of the top schools of his time. Barack made good use of the opportunities that were given to him. He managed to attend Columbia University after which he attended law school at Harvard (American Academy of Achievement, 2009).

In my regard, Barack Obama is the epitome of triumph over trauma in our lifetime. If you look closely within the lines of Barack Obama's history you will see a lot of blank spaces and gaps. These times show a colorful diversity of tragedy, challenges and limitations. Yet his life has paraphrased the definition of tolerance and determination. The blank spaces include the obvious absence of his father, partial insecurity on the part of his mother, genuine love and affection on the part of his grandparents and a big question sign of someone searching for identity on the part of the young child Barack.

Think of this young man who later hails from Chicago with roots in Hawaii, whose father is the descendant of Africa with roots in slavery, his mother an average white woman who married someone outside of her race during her college years when racism was at its peak. They divorced a few years later while he was still a toddler; thus starting his single parent episode. His mom at that time had to put her own livelihood on hold to grant her child the meager necessities to survive just like the average single parent of this time. His mother moved to Indonesia, remarried and sent the young child to live with his grandparents in Hawaii. His grandparents took on and tackled the task of providing his educational soundness.

I reflect on his inclusion in a totally white family when he came of age to realize that he was the only black person in the house. I gave thought to his childhood mind when he saw his mother pregnant with his sibling. He probably hoped with all his heart that the newborn would come with his skin color. He may have thought that would appease the supposed divide, however getting the unfortunate awakening that it was not so. His transition back to Hawaii could mean the replacement of stress and strain for tranquility in the house. That, however, did not hinder his collective persona to develop into the extraordinary man he is today.

   I do believe that the humility he now displays is a result of the experience and exposure that he captured and stored over the years from boy to adult life. I think it had to do partly with the back drop of hardship, disaster and immense emotional trauma that he had undergone.

   In his later years he must have seen loyalists fail and promises broken. He must have seen lives wasted and dreams dissolved. He must have undergone seasons of extreme drought for him to have such fervor to sacrifice career and opportunity after opportunity to become a public servant. Willingly choosing to fight for them that could not fight for themselves and fighting for those who hate him for the mere fact that he is black. He had to have divine protection to survive the age of greed when the get rich quick mentality was the order of the day. There is so much to say about this young man which we will do in the final chapter but he is proof that regardless of the situations that we arrive into, irrespective of the condition that we face; in spite of the causes that lurk in the shadows, we are all inexcusable. Failure should never be an option. There is no reason why we cannot make it in this life. We can do all things through Christ which strengthen us (Phil. 4:13). Yes we can!

# 2 Training

*And Pharaoh's daughter said unto her,
Take this child away, and nurse it for me,
and I will give thee thy wages.
And the woman took the child,
and nursed it.*
**Exodus 2:9**

♦ **Parental/Caregiver Training**

Mother's training is vital. We need parents and guardians who train children so that they can fulfill the "call of God" (designed destiny) in their lives. Parents and guardians have a significant role to play. Most times, the training of the children is in the hands of the mother because she generally spends more time with them in the early years. The types of children that are turned out into society are a direct product of the quality of training administered during the formative years. Esther was shaped by Mordecai, that prepared her to fulfill her role as Queen and then save the Jews from annihilation. The nameless damsel who danced and pleased the king, was shaped by her mother Herodias and she ended up asking for and receiving the head of John the Baptist on a platter (Matt. 6:25).

Jochebed was a God-fearing woman; she raised and fashioned her children Moses, Aaron and Miriam for greatness. Moses became the leader of the children of Israel; Aaron became the priest and Miriam a prophetess (Exod. 6:20-21).

Children are a heritage of the Lord...they are also like a quiver in the hand of a strong man (Ps. 127:3-4). This means that they will hit the mark wherever he fires them or go in whatever direction he channels them.

Have you ever heard some caring parents talking about their children? It probably goes something like this, "Oh! My child is on the honor roll in her class, oh she is so smart..." Did you ever notice that every proud parent speaks as if their children are the brightest? Have you ever heard a parent saying, "Oh! My child is a delinquent...he or she is good for nothing?" I hope not. But if you put your brilliant child among other brilliant children his or her own age, you may be surprised to know that your child may not be as brilliant as you make them out to be. Or if you make an inquiry into the juvenile probation list, you may see that the child that you thought was a delinquent or good for nothing is actually a very good child. This is to say that even while we celebrate our children and others "condemn", everyone must be modest and cognizant of the fact that every child needs direction. Every child has the choice of good or evil. Therefore, children need to be trained. Oops! I have just implied that our little angels have an inclination to imperfection. Don't be offended. Let me qualify that idea. In Elementary school when there was a fight, the rest of children would begin to shout and get excited while someone else got beat up. Children can be very mean and manipulative, some are bullies, some have fun by gossiping and name-calling and some even go further and harass others physically. Ultimately, children are shaped by context. That means we have to train up our children in the way that they should go, (way of the Lord) that when he is old he will not depart from it (Prov. 22:6).

Every parent must have insight into the lives of their children. They need an aspiration that will go beyond their present age, into the future and get a glimpse of their strategic placement and duties in the secular world. This will in turn cause parents to focus on the character development of their children.

Parents have to realize that God has great intentions for their children. Therefore parents should deal with their children from the standpoint that they are special. And special people should receive preferential treatment. The first teacher of a child is usually the mother. More than the school or social settings, the training of the mother and family will have a more lasting effect upon the child.

Today's parents seem to be quite liberal in child-rearing, they tend to extend borders and give children the opportunity to do as they like without correcting them. Some claim that it helps to develop autonomy. But this sort of permissiveness often leads to delinquency.

While we do not need to use authoritarian parenting styles, (demanding and not responsive to the needs of the child) we should use authoritative principles as it is proven to yield the best results.

Authoritarian parenting – A style of parenting in which parents rigidly control their children's behavior by establishing rules and valuing obedience while discouraging questioning…while authoritative parenting encourage verbal questioning, explain the reasons behind family policies, and sets limits (Kaplan, 2004). [sic]

The aforementioned treatment is not necessarily peaches and cream. Yet, it can serve as the building blocks of a firm character for our young ones. Most importantly, parents should not be silent and let children have their own way. The Bible refers to disciplining children in the following scriptures. You cannot spare the rod and spoil the child. Foolishness is wrapped up in the heart of a child but as Solomon says, the rod of correction will drive it out (Prov. 22:15). This does not condone child abuse. It is included to highlight the concept of discipline. For whom the Lord loveth he chasteneth (Heb. 12:6). Correction must be done with love.

There is a danger in subscribing to the philosophy of this time, in letting children do as they like. That danger is filling our jail cells and our courts with children committing 'adult' crimes. Not only should children have household rules, there has to be a moral code of conduct that directs the lives of our children.

Children must be taught the admonition and fear of the Lord. Teach them the 'Hebrew Shema' which says, "hear O Israel the Lord our God is one Lord" (Deut. 6:4). Both parent and child must only worship our God; Jehovah. Any other god is referred to as an idol. This can be anything in one's life that has the power to distract a person from godliness.

The Hebrew Shema was God's moral code or way amidst the ways of the world and the doctrine of polytheism to instill monotheism into the children of Israel. This thought process was rehearsed so much that there should not have been time for distractions. It was a dogmatic standard that fashioned the Israelites way of life.

The Shema did not only let it be known that Jehovah is the absolute and only God; the thought also placed dependency of the people upon God. The simple words of the Shema (Hear O Israel, the Lord our God is one Lord) had a greater implication than the plain words. It was a training of the minds to remain absolute to their purpose and calling in secular places. There was a faith-based dependency upon God through the meaning of the Shema. It relates to the suffixes attached to the name Jehovah. For example, Jehovah-Shammah means the Lord is present. Jehovah-Jireh the Lord will provide. Jehovah-Shalom God will grant us peace. All the previous suffixes and their subsequent meaning enhanced the belief and trust that the Israelites had in God.

If children learn initially that God is omnipresent, omnipotent and omniscient and that He is their sustenance along with the entire host of suffixes attached to Jehovah, they will reverence God and understand the depth of right and wrong. They will understand quite early who is King and who is the evil perpetrator and they will be able to shun the fruits of the flesh and abide by the fruits of the spirit. The verses following the Hebrew Shema in Deuteronomy further states that:

"...you should love the Lord with all thine heart and with all thy soul, and with all thy might. And these words that I command thee this day, shall be in thine heart, and thou shalt teach them diligently unto thy children, and shall talk of them when thou sittest in thy house and when thou walkest by the way, and when thou liest down, and when thou risest up. And thou shalt bind them for a sign upon thine hand, and they shall be as frontlets between thine eyes. And thou shalt write them upon the posts of thy house, and on thy gates" (Deut: 6:5-9).

The action of the scripture was a literal drill for the Israelites instead of a spiritual impartation. It was very concentrated in their camp as you will notice in the verses above and in similarity was taught to the next generation, rehearsed, digested, applied and lived in their uprising, down sitting, going out and coming in. Though this was didactic or moralistic, the Israelites said and believed, until it literally became a part of their system, mind and concepts.

When children are exposed in this sense to the presence and knowledge of the Lord they will develop a personal relationship with Him. And with the understanding that He is their keeper, protector, sustenance and guide, when they are old they will not depart from it, but will continue in righteous ways.

This was God's way back then to instill virtue and value and it was good for those people of that age; it is good and relevant for our children even in this day and age.

It is okay to have the knowledge that the Lord was with your parents but it is even better to know that the Lord is with you. Parents, you should personally expose your children to the knowledge of the Lord, you cannot depend on the school system alone; training must first begin in the home

We need mothers that can see something different in their children and will declare that they are Godly. We do not need parents that will declare doom and destruction when their children misbehave. Instead we need those that will correct them in love. We need mothers that though their children were exposed to the atmosphere of death, loss and mourning, they can still stand guard and not allow the atmosphere of destruction to penetrate the spirit of their children. We need parents and guardians who are determined to make it through difficult times and will not allow the difficult times to shape the nature of their children. Parents who through selflessness and determination, try to deliver the best for their child, will hide their weaknesses and pain behind smiles and cry deep into the nights. But the children will not see their tears nor hear their cries of pains until they are old enough to understand.

Society groans for parents that will bring their children to church and let them become a part of the body of Christ. Let them sleep in the pews or even on the carpets. It does not matter where they stay, as long as they are in church and the spirit of the Lord can seep into their spirit and permeate their entire being. When they get to where they belong in secular places they will know their God.

Consequently, when the enemy plays the music of worship to false gods they will not bend nor bow, instead they will lift their voices and declare that they only bow to Jehovah God, similarly, to the three Hebrew boys (Dan. 3:10-12).

It is the responsibility of all parents to teach their children about God because there will come a generation that does not know God: but if they know their God they will do great exploits (Dan. 11:32). The scriptures declare that if you know God you will be strong; therefore we have to train them to know about God and also to identify with themselves. They must know who they are. When Moses walked out of Pharaoh's house, many people saw him as an Egyptian but he knew who he was. We are a royal priesthood, who has been called out of darkness in to the marvelous light (1Pet. 2:9). Therefore, you must indoctrinate your child about their God and about themselves in the early years.

It is said of the Catholic Church, that if you give them a child from the ages of one to six years old and they train that child, the child will remain a Catholic for life. If this saying is true, then this must mean that the Catholics have a moral code that they use to fashion and concretize the minds of their young ones. In like manner, God has given you the opportunity to stabilize the faith and the mentality of your children so that when you release them into the world they will not change. The world will teach them evolution but they will know that God is still the creator, the world will teach them architectural skills but they will know that God is still the maker of all things; they can sit under the systems of the world's tutelage and still know their God. We have to expose our children to the ways of the world at every level. They must by all means be educated in schools at the highest level; they must know the thought process of intelligent people so that they can know what to bind and what to loose.

Let us take a general view into training up children in today's society. This by itself is serious business and may be considered to be one of the most important activities any parent may have to carry out. Some parents work very hard to make sure training their children is fun and as motivating as possible. However, training up children is more complicated today than it was many years ago. Not because parents are unable to carry out their duties effectively, but because society has set new standards and some moral values have drastically declined over the years. Also with the invention of new technologies and the evolving of current versions of the technologies, many parents find it very challenging to train their children according to what society demands and still maintain high moral values, ethical principles and rational thinking among their children. However, with the knowledge of right and wrong there is a base from which to train children.

To expound on the topic of a 'mother's training' towards the development of her children we must first establish a working definition. The view of who is a child varies from society to society according to culture, history and theories. International conventions define children as those aged 18 and under (What is child labor, 2009). However, in my opinion, a child may be considered to be a person from birth until he or she has reached adulthood in a given society. While being a child one's parents are solely responsible for his or her upbringing, and as such parents are expected to bring up their children with much love and affection. In most societies where oppression was once a part of the country's history, parental training was the main responsibility of the mother instead of both parents as often times the father is absent from the family, thus creating numerous situations of single parenting. In a quest to ensure that the children are brought up with good morals and ethical values, the mother from time to time would guide and direct the path of her own children. She would through selflessness, and often times self-denial make several sacrifices for her own children so that they would mature into worthwhile citizens, society would be grateful to receive.

When a woman has a baby she has to make the necessary adjustments to accommodate the new member of her family. In some cultures where the father is the main breadwinner and is often out working the mother is the main adult who has to train and discipline the children. Also in poor societies where only the fortunate and wealthy children attend school regularly, the mother is the main teacher. The children would regularly gather to listen to their mother as she gives her lectures in the form of stories and legends of their culture (Broude, 1995). On this premise, I therefore acknowledge the fact that mothers are often left with the responsibility to train up their children and are therefore expected to carry out this act with adequate efficiency. The job of training up children in an acceptable way by society is sometimes very difficult on the path of the mother.

However, most mothers carry out this task with pride and dexterity as they look toward the end result of the product which they will spend years to nurture.

A mother's training for her children may be divided into several stages so as to separately outline the need factor of each stage of development of the child. These stages will be adopted from Piaget's cognitive development of the child. The stages are as follows:

(1) From birth to age two - Sensory Motor Period,
(2) From age two to age seven - Pre-operational Stage,
(3) From age seven to age eleven - Concrete Operational Period,
(4) From age eleven to age fifteen - Formal Operational Period (Atherton, 2005). The division of the stages of the child's cognitive development is not absolute, but is a mere guideline for the purpose of explaining the duties of a mother during the training of her own children.

1. From the birth of a child until they are around age two there are some basic things a mother must do for that child to survive. In Piaget's ideas of child development, he stated that a child at this stage does not yet represent events mentally, but relies on coordination of senses and movement, (Atherton, 2005). John Locke also proposed that children were born "tabula rasa"... literally; "blank slate" (Uzgalis, 2007 -pp. 2.2

Book II) and that experience would determine what the infant became.

He maintained that education should be pleasant for the young child (Uzgalis, 2007). With a clear understanding of what Piaget stated and what Locke theorized, it can be said that mothers with children at this stage of cognitive development have the right and responsibility to nurture their children with maximum care. More often than not mothers would take the 'blank slate' and literally place information in it by just teaching, nurturing, reading, singing and caring for the children.

Children at this stage of development would normally have their mothers' breast feeding, cradling, and physically doing everything for them as they move from month to month in their development. Mothers are the child's first teacher before the child enters any formal school system. When children are about twelve months old, most of them begin to speak in complete sentences, imitate movements of other children and adults around them, display a full range of emotion, and test the limits of their primary caregiver. At this stage the mother will often point to the parts of the body and teach the child about their own body.

The child also knows where some objects are kept even if they are hidden from sight as they observe (Staszko, 2004). As the children grow older they become more aware of their environment and become curious to find out things on their own. Mothers with religious beliefs would also expose their children to their beliefs whether directly or indirectly through interacting with the children and by teaching them moral principles. This first stage of cognitive development is very crucial as the child observes, listens and stores information gathered through interacting with their mothers for future use in the developmental cycle.

2. Age two to seven which is labeled the Pre-operational Stage by Piaget, is said to be the stage at which children form many new schemas but do not think logically. The children have an ego-centric view of their world around them in terms

of their own perspective. It is also said that role playing begins at this stage (Atherton, 2005). A mothers' training for her child at this stage has become more complex as she now has to help the child think rationally and logically. It is now a mother's responsibility to make more informed decisions for the child. Children at this stage ask more questions than ever about things they see and hear.

Most mothers also potty train their children at the beginning of this stage as they prepare them for the formal school system or child care facilities. At this stage children are not logical thinkers, their actions or behavior will not reflect the thought patterns of children in the Concrete or Formal Operational Period. Mothers most often than not, will correct in love and may also have to discipline them according to their individual moral standards. Most times these moral standards are religiously-based, taken to be gospel and are consistently followed in order to get the best out of the children. Children at this stage will seek their mother's approval for things and will also desire help with things they believe their mother can help with. With this knowledge a mother can deposit bits of knowledge into the child's mental reservoir while attending to their needs.

3. From age seven to eleven which is referred to as the Concrete Operational Period by Piaget, is the period in which the child has internalized some physical tasks or operations and no longer depends only on what is visual, but begins applying logic to solve problems (Atherton, 2005). At this stage of the child's life he or she would have already been in Elementary school and would be exposed to influences from school and a wider society. A mothers' training now becomes more difficult as she has to also educate herself to keep up with the child's rapid developmental growth.

A mothers' training for her children is needed daily just as her attention to her child's every day needs. Children also look to their main caregiver for help in crisis and with problem solving. At this stage of cognitive development, physical development is also taking place with the children. Some children enter early puberty which is towards the latter end of this stage. Mothers will have to revamp and re-strategize their training methods to deal with the simultaneous physical and cognitive developments that are taking place with their children.

More often than not mothers are the ones who help their children with homework assignments, take the children to the parks, public library, church and other social gatherings for entertainment purposes. Because of this, an opportunity has been created for both mother and her children to bond both physically and emotionally, thus building up a level of trust between both parties. When children trust their mothers they will not be afraid to speak to them about any problems. The bonding between mother and their children accompanied by the existence of trust between both parties will serve as assets for years to come. When children are faced with crisis issues they will without delay turn to their mothers for advice and problem solving techniques because they trust them, and trust their judgment.

4. The fourth and final stage in Piaget's cognitive developmental stage of the child is called the Formal Operational Period and occurs in children between eleven and fifteen. This period, rare even in adults is characterized by sophisticated abstract thinking and logical reasoning abilities applied to physical, social and moral problems (Atherton, 2005). Children at this stage of cognitive development need guidance more than the forgone stages, as children are more seasoned in their teenage years. At this level of cognitive development both rapid physical development and actual changes are visible.

A mothers' responsibility to her children during the fourth stage of cognitive development is both complex and challenging. Mothers must now be caregivers, teachers, counselors and friends to their teenage children to assure a smooth transition from little children to young adults. With the astonishing revelation of the numerous problems teenagers face in today's world, which range from dealing with self identity, drugs, teenage pregnancy, and peer pressure, mothers have to be vigilant and sometimes aggressive in their approach when training their own children to become good moral citizens.

Piaget's Cognitive Developmental Theory is one of the most influential on early childhood education, as it describes how a child's thinking is unique in each of the four stages. For this reason this theory of cognitive development was chosen to help with the explanation of the role of mothers in the training of their children through the various stages of development. Mothers who are endowed with the responsibilities of training up their children (often times without the presence of a father) are expected to be cognizant of the various stages of development their children pass through in an effort to garner a better understanding of the principles on which training should be imposed, enforced or taught to the children in her care.

Mothers should be caring and supportive of their children. They should also be ready to listen carefully in order to understand their way of thinking, and analyzing the things around them that they see or hear. Mothers must also be ready to give explanations and correct their children if they have some erroneous concepts about any fact of life. Since most mothers are responsible for the training of their children they should teach them how to behave, react respectfully to controversial issues, and how to present their arguments on such issues. Mothers should be aware that teaching children in the early stages of their lives to deal with challenges, disagreements and problems in a respectful manner could prevent painful situations in the later stages of their lives due to disrespectful or out of control behavior. Again I say that the type of children turned out in society may be a direct product of the quality of training administered during the formative years of the children and is to be credited to the main caregivers whom at most times are the mothers.

Here are a few unclassified variables of a mothers' training from my mother's rule book blended with her stress alleviation pointers. (1) Turn off the television and read a book to and with your child every day. It will create a bond between parent and child and stimulate the intellectual development. (2) Teach your child the difference between need and want, requirement and desire and right and privilege in their everyday activities. This will give them a sense of value and appreciation. (3) Research and discuss family history, highlight generational disparity and compare and contrast the present and the past. This will preserve history and create a sense of respect for family and community. (4) Give your children household chores along with school home work and take the time to check when and how it's done. This will make them responsible and bring order and organizational skills to their lives. (5) Teach your child to clean-up after themselves. This is cleanliness. (6) Teach your child to use key words/phrases: such as please, thank you, excuse me and I am sorry. Manners and respect are the beginning of discipline. (7) Teach your children to save for future investment; it is essential to good stewardship. These are the measures and practices that my mom used as we were growing up. She can now boast that her present stress-free life is as a result of her past choices.

I believe that mothers try to do their best, given their means, challenges and circumstances and leave the rest to God to handle. Let us use Moses for our example to create a general picture. His mother was pregnant when the powers of the land were killing babies. She was in an atmosphere where everyone was a suspect; she had to keep herself hidden even from her neighbors.

It must have been difficult living with and nursing a baby in an atmosphere of suspicion. The cloud of secrecy finally gave way to the ingenuity Jochebed used to create Moses' ark. She insulated the ark with slime and set her baby afloat in the river of death; where the enemy would least likely suspect. The bond that she developed with her son was too great for her to allow him to be killed. Even when she set him afloat she refused to neglect him. She made sure someone looked out for him. Her love created a possibility for his destiny.

At this point, one has to reflect on a Mother's ability to protect and nurture what God has given them to bring forth. It is possible that the knowledge that "the earth is the Lord's and the fullness thereof the world and they that dwell therein" (Ps 24:1) allows so many mothers to work extremely hard to protect their children. In this day, abortion has become a choice. If you are reading this it is because your mother protected you to the best of her ability. Do not try to pass judgment on your mother or God because if you do not become bitter any situation will become better. That is why I can firmly say that your trauma could not destroy you. It was only a catalyst for your transformation. I have been in ministry long enough to know that "all things work together for good to them that love God, to them who are the called according to his purpose" (Rom. 8:28).

God has a way of coming to everybody's rescue and He will stop you from drifting into condemnation. He has a way of changing the tides and hoisting the larger sails to take you to the other side. And when you get there the past will fade into insignificance as it cannot be compared to the glory of the latter days. The high calling of mothers is one of utmost excellence and prestige in an intricate phenomenon of passage from the environment of death to start a child's secular training. It is not just a duty; it is a blessing, honor and a privilege for "Lo, children are an heritage of the Lord: and the fruit of the womb is his reward" (Ps. 127:3).

### ♦ Secular Training

Transition into college is usually the first major break from mother's environment into the outside world and this initially can be very exciting for some, while for others it is met with hesitation, intimidation, fear and speculation. This is usually an emotional moment when mommy's little ones have to go to a secular institution on their own for a lengthy period of time. However, growth comes with separation, exposure and new challenges. Here you are laying flat on your back in a bunk bed staring nonchalantly into an opaque ceiling reminiscing of the luxury of home. Your roommate blasting his music at an unconscionable volume, seemingly overjoyed, frolicking like a wild zebra celebrating his escape from the lions whelp, moments later he crashes below on the bunk, snoring like a motorcycle in the streets of Brooklyn.

The tiny room has inadequate spacing for one much more for two people and here you are in that position with a total stranger caged in an eight by ten convenience box probably for the next four years. At the break of dawn you are rushing to use the bathroom before the crowd, only to find that college never sleeps and the reality strikes that you are already late by the signs of the flooded bathroom floor and the stench of unflushed toilets.

At meal times you are eating cold slush at the cafeteria before you learn of the instrumental hotplate and fast food store down the block. A very emotional transition for both mother and youngster but here is where life will shape into prominence, here is where the world becomes smaller as your mind expands and you are exposed to the system of human thoughts and behavior as you gradually integrate into the diversity, and capture and secure knowledge and understanding. Here is where you align yourself with the fraternity and alumni and develop lasting and important relational ties.

The kings of the olden days and in particular the pharaohs boast of and took great pride in anyone "skilful in all wisdom, cunning in knowledge, and understanding science, and such as had ability in them to stand in the king's palace..." (Dan. 1:4). These kings trust in astrology and relied heavily upon magicians and sorcerers and young people with intelligent minds apt to teach and sway them into these and more sophisticated endeavors. This is the stage at which high society engraft these young men and women to cement them in the way that they deem necessary. These young brilliant minds usually transmit a fresh perspective and depth of wisdom; they are usually pragmatic and proactive. It is at this time and standard that they are needed most by both sides of the spiritual aisle. This is the time when identity matters most and choices are increasingly significant.

Denying oneself of a college education can be detrimental to the fulfillment of our purpose. You won't discover how smart people think. You will be unprepared to bind principalities and powers if you are not proportional to their league. You will be unable to bind the strongman and spoil his goods if you do not know the ways of the strongman. God will not strategically place you in society if you have no knowledge of society. The knowledge of God can't cover the earth if we remain in a religious box. If you train your child well they will not be changed by the system, hence there should be no fear of knowledge. Being educated or knowledgeable of the sorcerers and witchcraft does not mean endorsement of same, evil may enter the eyes but that does not mean that it entered the soul. I dare say that while we learn from experience and exposure we do not give ourselves to idols neither do we glory in the knowledge of man.

Peer pressure will dissolve into nonexistence when individuals truly identify with themselves. Moses proved that years ago, the scripture says, "By faith Moses, when he was come to years, refused to be called the son of Pharaoh's daughter; Choosing rather to suffer affliction with the people of God, than to enjoy the pleasures of sin for a season" (Heb. 11:24-25). He could without much resistance say to our day, 'I pass' to alcohol, drugs and sexual sins. Hence, it can be fairly stated that he esteemed the reproach of Christ greater riches than the treasures of Egypt. We are no different from Moses, in fact we are liken unto Jesus Christ, being a part of his body. Education causes us to have leverage, good sense of values, strength of character and confidence. We are able to distinguish between temporal and eternal. We learned quite early that a position in the kingdom of the earth is temporary but a position in heaven is eternal, we can see beyond our horizon. We can look far beyond the knowledge of the world, because we do not lay our affection on things on this earth but on things above (Col. 3:2).

At this time secular training gears the participant for warfare because you no longer see from a limited point of view, you are able to see the whole picture. You will now be exposed to spiritual wickedness in high places and will see the implication it has on the minority. You will have the opportunity to see into the closet of great men and see them for who they really are. The scales will fall from your eyes and as you observe, you will begin to feel people's hurt and absorb their pain and your spirit will yearn for answers and solutions.

Training will gradually increase to new levels, preparing and propelling you into areas that only God could carry you to and keep you in. There you will be met with harsh realities and much resistance. Because the world will ask, who are you and who is your God that they should obey Him? While the world desperately desires your expertise, they will resent your very presence to the core. While you bring the companies viable ideals and increase profits on all fronts they will coin ways to keep you at a depraved level so that they can manipulate you. This will occur not because of your attitude or moral standing but because you are in training.

When I was in banking, I use to work as a System Business Analyst. The job was quite challenging but being disciplined I arrived early and stayed late at the bank to ensure that all the work was done in a timely manner and to the satisfaction of the clients. The clients were satisfied, volumes increased and my sacrifice was noted. My manager became quite threatened of my work ethic and ability and refused to give me the necessary recommendation for a salary increase, even though the work that I did was twice the amount that everyone else did. I was receiving the lowest salary in my grade.

Instead of a recommendation, the manager began to inform me of all the negative issues that surrounded the hierarchy, and why he believes that I will not get an increase. When he realized that I would not bend he said to me in plain English, "Barry, I think that you should leave this company and go elsewhere and find yourself a job, because as long as I am here as your manager you will never be promoted." I sent out my resume and within two weeks I received three job offers, each with a better salary and benefits than I was receiving at the bank. The following Monday morning, I wrote my resignation letter and took it to the office with the intention of handing it to my manager, but I was told that he was out for the day. I thought of going up the ranks to hand in the letter, but on second thought I decided to wait until the next day as I wanted to give it to him personally, when he came to work. He never showed up the next day either, we heard later that he was sick and hospitalized. A few days later he died. The Vice President came to me and said, "Barry, the ball is now in your court." I told him that I was handing in my resignation letter because I had found another job and was only waiting on my manager to return to give in the letter. The VP informed me that I was the driving force of the department so he will not accept it. I asked him, why this was not communicated to me before; he let me know that they had discussed this with my manager. They had informed him, even though he kept me ignorant and insisted that I leave. Ironically, the manager was right when he said that I could not get a promotion while he was there. Before he was buried my salary was put on par with the rest of my league, I was promoted to his position and my salary doubled.

I want to let you know that the world will notice that your methodology is seamless and they will be attracted. They will see that there is something different with the way you respond when you are under extreme pressure and they will envy your composure, thoughtfulness and thorough approach though it is to their benefit.

At this time more than ever you have to learn relational skills. You have to learn to bridge the divide and work both sides of the aisle. Partisanship will be to your detriment because whether you believe it or not at this point of training true friendship is a rare commodity. Those that are closest to you are the ones who will deny and betray; they are the ones that will backbite and stab, they are the ones who will smile and nod and deep in their hearts they are ravening wolves. You will have to learn the true craft of relational skills and master it to survive. You will have to learn how to be at peace with all men if possible and strike a compromise without asking for a truce. You will have to take advantage of common ground.

Winning a battle does not mean that you have won the war. You may have to side step the land mines of grievous words that stir up anger and resist the anger that rest in the bosom of fools. You must by every means necessary passionately present your soft answer and let the anointing drive away the wrath of men. Later on you will learn that there are some battles that are just not worth fighting. Hence, sometimes you have to slight a conversation without being cynical, and run to survive. You have to know when to give specifics and when to give generalized answers so that it does not return to haunt you. Most of all you have to learn to remain in the borders of your delegated confines. You have to learn how and when to give up your right for the sake of peace, for the saving of souls and for the better good.

Everybody knows that the coin has three sides and so does every tale, my side, your side and the truth. I submit it to you this way, that the coin has three sides - two flat sides and a round one. You do not have to always settle a conversation the same day, time is a rebounding tool and what goes around will come around. Strength of mind or brainpower is always better than muscles and to the greater thinker belongs the greater prize.

Always remember that strength is not measured by might but experience teaches wisdom. Everything is a cycle. Just like biological cycles in plant and animals, it is no different within the cycles of life; the cycle begins exactly where it ends. From the dust we came and to the dust we shall return. Some things that people fight so hard over, some things that they connive and kill for, some things that influence people to step on each other to achieve, in forty years from now it will lose its savor and become distasteful and irrelevant. However, the offender will have to live with their conscience and the traumatic scars of recompense. The dramatics are brought to naught when we remember that, "...Whatsoever man sows that shall he also reap" (Gal. 6:7). The world will not always accept love but there is no law against it, therefore while in training please use love as your measuring stick.

This portion of training is what I call "terrain training." To appreciate it fully you will end up drawing from all your reservoirs of knowledge from childhood to college, from trauma to training and still come up short. Then you will find that intuition and your value system will kick in and the reality will make true the saying that some leaders are born but some are terrain bred.

The initial life of Joseph between the time of trauma and training was no different either. The traumatic experience of living among his envious brothers was hard enough for him and we also know he made it more difficult at one point by being a "blabber mouth." He reported his brother's evil deeds to their father but what on earth could cause your own flesh and blood to see you coming afar off to enquire of their wellbeing; and plot on how to kill you when you come near? Can envy be so strong that his very family calls him by his talent in a demeaning way instead of by his name? They announced him as 'here comes the dreamer.' This was not done as a compliment, it was indeed sarcasm. They hated him to the core because he had the audacity to talk about his dream.

Visualize their conversation,"...he is only seventeen and he thinks that he is our deliverer, who does this little halfwit think he is...." They devoured him with their words and reduced the definition of his character until anger permeated their thoughts and the fangs of death were their ultimate resolution.

What could have possessed them to strip their brother of his identity and cast him naked into a pit and have the gall to tell their father that some evil beast killed him (Gen. 37:18-20)? This aspect of his trauma was a classic textbook style of training. The scripture did not say how long the brothers stayed in the field before returning home and it certainly did not say how long Joseph stayed in the pit before they sold him to the Ishmaelites. It never spoke of the depth of the pit or how dark and cold it was but we can all tell that he was hurting silently with deep uncovered wounds, he was ailing tremendously in a pit of doom.

No one would listen to his plea, no one cared to understand his cries. He was not the villain or a vagabond, yet he was neglected, rejected and disrespected by everyone. I visualized his days dim and his night's dark with not even a flicker of light much less a spark. I can see him naked and cold in the desert night questioning himself asking how he got in the darkness and depth, narrow and queer, but, "Beloved, think it not strange concerning the fiery trial which is to try you, as though some strange thing happened unto you" (1 Pet. 4:12). I told you earlier that the ones closest to you are the pulse of your descent but that is not for you to become paranoid because as Samson says, "out of the eater came forth meat, and out of the strong came forth sweetness..." (Judg. 14:14). The thing that intended to kill you shall bless you. You will be rewarded in due season if you faint not (Gal. 6:9). Soldiers need wars to shine as leader's need disasters to soar.

Hard as this may sound, there has to be a trigger finger to push you into formation, there has to be a Judas to sell you out for little or nothing so that you will know that your help comes from above. There has to be a Peter who will disassociate himself and deny the very existence and knowledge of his alignment with you so you can travel to the furnace by yourself. You have to sit on that potter's wheel in the fire all by yourself with the colorful collection of the thoughts of your demise. Here you will have no handle of opportunity for escape, only to wait upon the course of nature because you are in training and the training must be completed by all or any means necessary.

Many believers and Christians in particular think that because they have the Holy Ghost and are already gifted and anointed, they do not need training. They are misinformed. There are many situations that will arise that they need to be trained to handle. Here are some questions to answer: How will you react when principalities and powers are released against your life if you are not trained? What account will you pull from when you are under extreme pressure and have limited time to react? What will you do when the lives of men are in your hands? What do you do when you follow the guidelines and call for the elders of the church to pray for a loved one and the loved one dies? What do you do when your back is against the wall and seemingly Jesus did not show up? What will you do when you are in the coliseum of death and the crowd roars at your downfall and the scorners quote scriptures that warrant your death? What do you do when those that you thought would stand for you begin to distance themselves to save their reputation? When, through dazed vision, you look up into the stands of the coliseum and all you can see seems like a uniformed choir pleading, crucify him… crucify him and you cringe with pain as the sound crescendos into your ear. What will you do? What will the course of your thoughts be when you are stripped of esteem and robbed of worth, sold out and locked up? What will your thoughts be when you are deprived of hope and filled with despair while uncertainty and fear looms in the air? What will your thoughts be when all men hate you and they will not speak peaceable unto you?

Training helps you to become disciplined and make those difficult decisions. Training will teach you to encourage yourself in the Lord. Training will tell you to stand still and see the salvation of the Lord. Training will cause you to make unpopular decisions that will bring justified results. Training will cause you to weigh and calculate situations; think quickly and act appropriately. Training will let you know that it is ok to fail; it's ok to lose for defeat is not death and delay is not denial. This is the point that distinguishes travel agents from tour guides, this is the point at which great leaders and warriors are made. Here is where the great will say I have fought a good fight and have kept the faith but the course is not finished. Here is where the trainee usually sees the crack or the slight ray of hope which when capitalized on, will cultivate strength within. That is the strength that will take you to victory's shore and like Paul you can then say I have finished the course.

Then the naysayers' sarcasms will have no impact on you and you will learn and add new meaning to songs like… "through it all, through it all I have learned to trust in Jesus I have learned to trust in God." Job when he had come to the knowledge of the purpose of his position said, "Though he slay me, yet will I trust in him (Job 13:15) and when the reality sets in, he concluded that, "…all the days of my appointed time will I wait till my change come"(Job 14:14). Training helps you to realize, during your demise, God kept you.

For example, when we came to New York, I could not get back into banking as easily as I thought that I would. But I thought that I had enough money to last until we were settled in. Unfortunately, we were hit by some unexpected eventualities that totally depleted our finances. As a result, I temporarily worked for an agency.

One day the agency sent me to a lady's office to pack some boxes for a moving truck. At the time I considered the job very mediocre and I was very frustrated at my calamity, as I could not walk away from it because I needed the money. I literally cried deep within myself as I went and packed the boxes, however, I labeled and put them into sequence, and thoroughly cleaned up afterwards without her asking me to. The lady was so impressed that she told me that she would ensure that I would be paid the equivalent of one week's pay for the two days that I worked. I thanked her and left, thinking that was the end of the ordeal and that I would not get a week's pay. But, I did receive the salary that she promised me and on top of that she called the agency to inform them that she was extremely pleased with the job that I had done. (I later learned that this was a woman that the agency described as "not being able to please"). The next week she sent for me personally to come and unpack the boxes and though still ego-bruised, I worked diligently...asking God, why? During casual conversation with her I found out that she was a prominent person in the banking industry. Without reservation, she gave me a recommendation that preceded my presence in the industry. Everyone in the office began to ask; who is this Goldson? She became my way back into banking.

Because of her recommendation every person that came to the agency in search of a job and used my name as a reference got the job...about twenty people at one point. My word to you is, whatever you do, do it as unto God. You never know where it will lead you, what purpose is wrapped up in it, and who will help propel your purpose and lead you to your call.

Stay under the hand of the Lord until your change comes. Do not abort the process. Soldiers say that the more you sweat in training the less you will bleed in wars. So do not be afraid of the devil's devices because he cannot kill you. God had already sent the drought that there should be no water in the pit for

Joseph, He is doing the same for you. He has already made a way to preserve you long before you get here. There is a sacred call on your life and that's what made you into the survivor that you are. God has already disarmed the enemy, there is no teeth in the enemies' mouth to bite, their hands have no claws, their guns have no real bullets, their swords are dull and their feet are not strong enough; neither can they stay long enough on your neck to hold you down because you are chosen for an assignment and your training has to be completed. You are destined for victory!

Even from your solitary confines of the pit you can still look up and see the stars of the almighty God and that in itself is a signal of hope that you can still lift up your eyes unto the hills, from whence cometh your help (Ps. 121:1).

Joseph's brothers thought that it was the end of him when they sold him as a slave to the Ishmaelites but they were only the conduit of his transition. He was now into an environment that he would not have gone into if they had not hated him. His prison in the pit, nakedness and hunger was a firsthand experience of what the people that he was destined to help would encounter. The world was naked, cold and hungry though they knew it not and he was sent there to procure clothing, food and the amenities to sustain life.

From this point, going forward in the life of Joseph, he had uncommon favor, great access and power. This is a relative reflection of everyone at this stage of training though the feeling will seem as passive confinement. Here, whether or not it is a pit or a prison the favor will be divine. The Potiphar of your life will see greatness in you and will promote you over his entire house (Gen. 39:4). You will begin to see the world from a new vantage point with the ability to effect minor changes at this time and though the people in your circles will be intimidated and fearful of your presence, you will have learned how to make allowance for them.

Your presence will command ultimate submission and relative reverence and they will be fearful, partly because they will be able to discern that in time you will become their superior. They will fear your ability to organize and mobilize men and women to execute great ambitions with minimal means, and as a result they will try to contain and enslave you. Because of your ingenuity they will be fearful that you are going to become more lucrative than them and that you will join allegiance with their enemies to displace them.

As you approach touching distance of a place of prominence the roller coaster ride will begin, battles will appear as if they are more heated and directed personally at you, but by now you should realize that it is a God thing, and it is God enhanced.

Everything in your life is a result of God's blessing. The lesson you will learn here is that it is God who gives the ability to create wealth. Although the system authorizes your pay check and signs off on your promotion, you ought to know in your spirit that it was God that blessed you and not your boss, because promotion does not come from the east nor from the west but from God. Therefore the secret of your success is dependent upon what you place in God's hand, for He will take little and make it much.

You have to realize that your blessing came from the hand of a man but before it reached the hand of a man it first came out of the hand of God and when the medium or conduit is taken out of the way the source is still present. God can take people out of your life that once was a blessing and you will remain blessed. So while you celebrate people that are in your life do not cry when they are taken out of the way because you still have a God that lives and you are going to be blessed. You will multiply and increase in the land because God has already written out your spiritual script. With or without man's help you are going to be blessed. It doesn't matter who or what dies, you are going to live so don't lose your peace because men are perplexed and famous people are taken out of position, your source is God. Celebrate people but don't fixate on them. You will discover that it is God who will prosper you and that He will prosper you where ever you go. It does not matter if you are in the pit or in Potiphar's house you are going to be blessed by God.

Sometimes, the people will let the system work for them and seemingly against you. You have to learn now that you are not going to be in slavery the way it was back then, so do not be ignorant. Be cognizant that while you are climbing the hierarchal ladder of success, while you are there as if you are next door to heaven; they are plotting how to destroy you. Hence, you are to watch and pray, you are to worship with one hand and guard with the other; you have to be attired in the whole armor of God daily.

People will not understand that you have been blessed by God to preserve their lives. They will not know that you are not an oppressor and that you are not there to kill and to destroy. Instead, you are there to be of assistance and to enhance their spiritual and socioeconomic wellbeing.

Initially they will not see the value that you are adding to their economy. Not everyone will readily appreciate the contribution that you made to society and to save their lives. Some people will look at you and underestimate your importance to their lives. They do not know that it is because of you that they are surviving and they will think that if they increase the pressure you will die; but you must make room for their doubting and misgivings, you must make allowance for people to grow.

Therefore you have to display an elegant approach that they will know that if you move into an environment that they deem secure and you adjust their comfort zone, they will know that you never came to destroy but to complement and make it better. If you approach areas that they hold sacred, they need to know that you are not there to devalue but to add value to it. They will learn soon enough that if you get into their educational facilities, you are going to lift it to higher standards.

Pretty soon they will know that if it was not for your help they would not have the empire and prosperity that they presently enjoy. They will realize in time that you are the wind beneath their wings; they will realize that they have been standing on your shoulders and you were aware and were happy to be their support because part of your assignment was to improve and preserve their life.

At this time however, when everything seems to be under control your tranquility will be disrupted again, lest you think that you have reached your optimum goal. The devil will see your steady progression and once more he will intervene to damage your character and credibility. Like Joseph, the catalyst will react in Mrs. Potiphar (sexual attack) and she will be attracted to you. She will be like the devil incarnate, a viable tool for the devil to try to make a total mockery to God and your ministry.

She will be fair to look upon, sleek with charming presumptuousness and flattering lips to seek your heart. She will be so confident of your cooperation that she will prepare a bed decked with tapestry and fine Egyptian linen richly perfumed in myrrh, aloes, and cinnamon and then she will extend her invitation to induce your demise. "... for she hath cast down many wounded: yea, many strong men have been slain by her. Her house is the way to hell, going down to the chambers of death (Prov. 7:26-27). Have you noticed that in our society, sexual perversion is a major obstacle that destroys a lot of our prominent men? This is not unique to our time. It caught King David, it messed up Judah and as strong as Samson was it lured him into self destruction. But the devil is a liar; you have greater power than the seductive powers of the adversary. God has given everything into your hands and you have the ability to tell him/her no! You ought to behave yourself wisely in the house of Potiphar, you do not have to unbutton your shirt and show your chest, you do not have to flex your muscles, you do not have to show your cleavage and lift your skirt to get there. It was not your sexuality that initially caused them to be attracted to you, they were attracted because they sensed the call of God upon your life and there is a spirit behind the attraction that is trying to get you out of the will of the Lord. So you must learn to control hormones and tell the devil to 'look but don't touch', tell the devil to go ahead and desire but he cannot have.

When you do not align yourself with the enemy's promiscuity plans or whatever device that is brought against you, they are going to lie on you but their lying will not define neither will it reflect your identity. You may be persecuted for the lie, found guilty and sent into solitary confines because there is someone attached to the king in the same dungeon that you must meet. He will be a confirmation of your transition to the palace but he will not directly help you. In fact, your contact in prison will have amnesia concerning your regards. God himself will have to rock the boat of authority to deliver you as your help can only come from the Lord.

From this point onward your patience and your trust in God will rapidly increase as you will learn from your previous pitfalls to prominence that God will not leave you neither will He forsake you. You will learn like David that if you ascend up into heaven, He is there and if you make your bed in hell, He is also there (Ps. 139:8).

No one will need glasses and or spiritual eyes to see that everywhere you went you were blessed, it will be quite evident. Because when you were sold to the Ishmaelites you were not resold to an ordinary person you were resold to the king's chamberlain in the form of Potiphar who favored you. When you went to prison you did not go to the regular jail, you were in the king's prison where the king's servants were kept and you were favored by the keeper of the prison. Though you were at the bottom, you were at the top of the bottom and pretty soon you will be at the top of the top. Regardless of the pitfalls, your ascension is inevitable!

In these situations help will always come from the least expected places, the least expected people and at an unexpected time. It is not going to come from the people that you have helped in your lifetime neither will it come from your associates and friends but it may come from a stranger or your very enemy. The same people that threw Joseph into the pit were the same ones that God used to pull him out. This is the reason why you have to use love as your measuring stick in dealing with everyone because you will never know the one that God is going to assign to deliver you from the gutters. This will teach you that although you are despised by many, you are not hated by all. There is a silent set unknown to you, but appointed by God to help you. These people are not usually among the crowds that give praise, they are not in need of a pat on the back, they are simply happy to be a part of the vision of the Lord and they always remain incognito.

They may not be of the eloquent bunch but they have a unique talent that is vital to your survival. They usually throw themselves headlong into your cause even in the face of death. God will always bless them tremendously. Just like the midwives who did not participate in Pharaoh's annihilation plans; God built them houses right there in Egypt. The Pharaoh was duped into believing that these people were doing evil to their Israelite women and God was still blessing them, but that was not so. They threw themselves into the saving of souls and had not laid their hands against the Lord's anointed neither did they do his prophets any harm. They left off building their own homes to protect the people of God, therefore God built them houses. You will learn along the way that when you help and support God and His people He will in turn help and support you. There is no way to lose when you throw in your lot on the side of God.

◆ **Priestly Training**

I found out that sometimes when good people are in a predicament that is uncaused by them, it is geared to place them into a temporary place of hold to hide them from the devil. This way they can be in touch with the true essence and power of their giftedness. This place of hold could be interchangeably called a valley, the backside of the mountain or a desert land. It is a place designed for you to meet and take a lesson from the priest and ultimately God. The scripture says that though you walk through the valley of the shadows of death that God will be there with you (Ps. 23:4). Therefore, valleys of predicament are for the refinement of giftedness.

Everyone that is called by the Lord has to spend time in the backside of the desert or valley, allow God to purge them from the world and train them to handle a sacred affair in a secular environment regardless of their academia. Trainees have to be pushed into an unfamiliar environment or valley that they neither have the stealth nor versatility to maneuver in order to get the quintessence of their character.

Before Joseph was sold into slavery in Egypt, the scripture only recorded him dreaming, it never spoke of him interpreting dreams. He would tell his dreams to his family and they would interpret it. They were all Hebrews who had similar cultural orientation and beliefs. So they could compare a reflected course of nature in a dream and interpret the application that was relevant to them. For example, Joseph told his brothers this dream where they were all binding sheaves in the field and Joseph's sheaf arose and stood upright and his brothers' sheaves stood round about and made obeisance to his sheaf (Gen.37:7). His brother immediately interpreted the dream by asking, "…Shalt thou indeed reign over us? or shalt thou indeed have dominion over us" (Gen. 37:8)?

"And he dreamed yet another dream, and told it his brethren, and said, Behold, I have dreamed a dream more; and, behold, the sun and the moon and the eleven stars made obeisance to me. And he told it to his father, and to his brethren: and his father rebuked him, and said unto him, what is this dream that thou hast dreamed?" Shall I and thy mother and thy brethren indeed come to bow down ourselves to thee to the earth" (Gen. 37:9-10)?

Now here is Joseph into his valley of predicament in the king's prison in Egypt with men of different cultures and moral values, men whose lifestyles define idolatry, men who were exposed to astrology, sorcery and witchcraft. These men had dreams that did not align with the course of nature that Joseph was used to, so that he could easily identify a parallel pattern for interpretation. It was an unfamiliar portrait yet immediately he could tell them the interpretation with ease and relaxation. Why? Because valley situations sharpen insight, enhance revelation and prepares you for bigger eventualities that will be imminent. Valley experiences are priestly. Though the interpretation was correct, their dreams were not just to get one killed and the other restored as interpreted, it was so designed to get Joseph out of prison.

In the valley your soul will find restoration, the light of Jesus will illuminate your spirit and you will develop the sharp senses and keenness of a shepherd. You will become vigilant, protective and innovative. The valley experience will teach you compassion for all men because you will identify with their situation in your valley and this will help you to look beyond faults and see needs. It will teach you not to capitalize on their weaknesses but to teach with kindness and patience. You will learn how to communicate orders at scheduled intervals clearly and concisely using a simple language that is easily understood. "For if the trumpet give an uncertain sound, who shall prepare himself to the battle" (1 Cor. 14:8)? Jesus says; my sheep hear my voice. Likewise you will learn how to deliver a clear sound word to the people of God so that they can be delivered from their circumstances.

The scriptures use the word sheep interchangeably with the word people. Relatively, if you are going to lead sheep you have to learn the purpose of the rod and the staff which is an insignia of sovereignty and grace by which you will rule over the people of God with care and concern.

Every family has a circle of trust and an environment of belonging, and so will the people that are under your care. This place of trust is a premise where families can let their hair down and relax, a place where they do not have to "dot I's and cross T's" a place where you can be open without fear and embrace purity and feel comfortable and secure. In the animal kingdom, the lion in particular would walk around the pride land and urinate on trees to stake claim and mark borders. Should a stray beast or other evil perpetrator come near, then the lead lion would alert the rest of the pride and defend the family. Likewise you will learn how to train the people that will be under your care to acquire a sense of smell for home and family. In so doing, when they go astray and hurt themselves, which they will, on their return, you will not condemn nor condone. Instead, you will provide therapy and keep them in the confines of righteousness so that they can feel the closeness of God and develop a sense of trust that they will not go wandering off again. If not, you will be tending the ninety and nine and forget that there is one out in the cold. I always tell my colleagues that I am called to the Gentiles, that is, the "unchurched", the man in the streets or the 'one' that is not a part of the fold. I never believed they could be won by only using pious means and theological text. I learned quite early from my relationships with the Salvation Army and the Catholics (who have a tremendous thirst for community service) that in order to get to them you have to meet them where they are at. You have to approach them at the core of their perception and need.

Everyone wants their children to grow up in a safe community, and be educated in a comfortable environment that is conducive to learning. Senior citizens need to know that if they get sick and the hospitals cannot afford them, there is a person that cares and is able to provide them refuge. Jobs need to be available. Grants and scholarships need to be available that those who need it can access it with ease and contentment. Quality of life must always be at the upper end and the incarcerated must be reconciled and start rehabilitation before they re-enter society that once again they can become contributing citizens. These measures and ambitions are not unique to governments and are not their responsibilities only. It is also the responsibility of those that are called by God. Most of the people that fit these needs are the 'one' that are not yet a part of the fold. God is concerned about the ninety and nine but He is also concerned about the one that is lost. God takes particular interest in the needs of individuals.

Sheep like people are simple, therefore, one has to learn to lead them in a simple way. You have to learn to shear them, expose their inner gifting and talents and help them to develop it. In the same breath, you have to learn how to use the two-edged sword; you have to learn and know when to make an incision to allow healing and when to amputate in order to save the body, you have to know when to clean for cleansing sake and when to clean cut for separation.

The priest will take you from the shepherds' identity to a Godly index and there you will to learn how to administer sacrifices and how to create an atmosphere for God's presence at any given moment with worship, reverence and fear. You will learn of the laws and ordinances, those that are written on the fleshy parts of the heart and those that are embedded on tables of stone. You will learn the sacredness of the altar and you will see the beauty of the Lamb on the throne and you will learn the practicality of Christendom that it does not become burdensome. Whatever you do you have to remain under the covering of a man of God, there has to be a rearguard of protection while you are on battle fronts or in your entire endeavor.

All this is happening in the back side of the desert away from the publics' eye, hidden from distraction. Then the ultimate thing will happen…the priest will teach you the solemnity of approach to the presence of God and the demeanor to be portrayed whenever you are in his presence because of the knowledge of his awesome greatness.

The priest will tell you the rituals of access but God will say come boldly to the throne of grace. The priest will tell you to go from the altar of sacrifice to the laver before entering the Holy Place and the Holy of Holies. But God will say come let us reason together, though your sins be as scarlet, they shall be as white as snow. This is not to contradict the priest because all that God is saying is wrapped up in the priest's instruction; it is God's way of extending the invitation personally to alleviate fear, in the same breathe. You will learn from the priest that the mannerism that you portray when having a conversation with your parents will be totally different from the one that you will have with the Lord. This means that if you were to have a conversation with your friends, the same conversation would have a different aura if you were talking with your parents or with the president. Likewise the approach to the Lord should have superior distinction than that which would pertain to the priest, parents or the president, this means that there is a protocol to be trained in when speaking to or approaching God. God has ways, statues and precepts. You have to know what to put on when you are going before God and it is different from what you wear before pharaoh.

◆ **God's Training**

When you come into the presence of the Lord all the training that has preceded Him will fade into insignificance. Just to behold His presence will shift your spirit into a dimension that is unspeakable. One touch of the hem of His garment will transform your darkness into light, your misunderstanding into understanding and your fear into faith. As a trainee you will understand Him the way Moses knew Him. You will understand the "burning bush" and that message will be embedded deep into your spirit for a lifetime (the bush was burning but not consumed). You will understand that though the people of God were afflicted they still grew to be a strong nation that brought fear into the eyes of their slave masters. Though their hands were callus and sore and their backs bruised they multiplied greatly, meaning that God was there and He kept them amidst their trauma. Wherefore when you go to deliver this people it is not you who are doing the delivering, you are only a conduit. There is a God that is bigger than life in your spirit, hence the glory will always be unto the Lord and not to a man.

The burning bush is there to let you know that these people that you are going to are in bondage but they are kept by God; they were in the fire but were not consumed. The people that you are going to are people that God has protected and set aside, therefore, no weapon formed against them shall prosper. God has spoken of their destiny from the foundation of the world and He is a covenant-keeping God. Even though they are in slavery He still kept them. He issued the commandment for them to be blessed and they shall be blessed. The burning bush experience is there to remind you that God will not back out on His words; He is not a man that he should lie nor the son of man that He should repent. If He said he will do it, He is going to make His promise good. They are destined for good, the strength of Israel shall not lie, says Jeremiah. For with God there is no variableness nor shadow of changing. He is reliable.

He is dependable and his words are forever settled in heaven; so let God be true and every man a liar.

The burning bush is there for you to know that before you go out and think that you are responsible for their deliverance you must know that God is theirs and your strength. Before you go God will have you to know that they have been in prison for hundreds of years but they have not been forgotten; the time may be long but God has not forgotten. Their tasks have been great but all they need to do is to hold on because He has seen the affliction of His people and Has come down to deliver them. God sees, hears and knows and He is come down to deliver. It will not be Moses neither will it be the person assigned in the secular places. Peter in the New Testament was quick to clarify this when he performed a healing and the people tried to glorify him, He said, "... Ye men of Israel, why marvel ye at this or why look ye so earnestly on us, as though by our own power or holiness we had made this man to walk" (Acts 3:12). So before you go you have to know that God will be for you the I Am that I Am. The I Am that I Am will be the deliverer.

### ♦ Learning To Wait On Your Sacred Call

After you have seen and have received the revelation of the burning bush there is a waiting period for the final word from God before the assignment. He is not going to send you out without telling you the outcome. He is the author and the finisher, and He knows the way that you go before you go. He just wants to assure you that no matter what you go through there is guaranteed victory at the end.

Therefore, when you step out of the secular training, and before you take on God's assignment you have to remember the critical factor that timing is of utmost importance. Paul says we must wait on our ministry. Not because you are educated, not because you have identified your call and not because you know God, means that you are ready. You have to learn how to wait on God's time or you will end up in trouble. You will fight battles that you ought not to be fighting, you will interfere with issues that you have no God given right to handle. You must understand that not every situation that you are confronted with will need you to provide a solution. Every fight does not need a fix. Some fights you will have to learn to ignore and wait until God tells you that here is a battle that He wants you to fight. You will get into trouble if you step out of timing. There is a time and season that the Lord has you wrapped up into. Even though you think you are ready, you still have to wait upon God. Yes you are gifted, called, anointed, trained and educated but you still have to wait upon the Lord. Your back may be bending or your knee might be wobbling; your hair may be gray but you still have to wait upon the Lord. If not, you will kill folks before their time and you will ultimately face rejection instead of acceptance. You cannot help people that do not know that they need help. Neither can you help those that God does not send you to help. Even though they need food it will not make sense for you to provide it unless you know that they are going to eat it. One has to be quick to hear and slow to speak. You have to know how to hold back your hand until they need your help.

You may be saved but that does not give you the right to meddle into everybody's problem. You have to listen to the voice of God and hear what God has called you to do or you will end up frustrated. God knows the right place to send you to and He knows the right time, and nobody can hold back what God has predetermined, decreed and declared for your life when He sends you. Therefore you are to celebrate God for where you are right now and do not be anxious for anything but in everything give thanks. Do not be dismayed and don't complain about where you are because that is the pivotal point for your next move towards your destiny.

Then when the time is right God will saturate the ground of your deployment and tell you to go. He will do the reconnaissance by himself and let you know that the course is clear; He has already prepared the hearts of men to accept you. Those who will resist, He has given you power over them. They are there just to keep you fit and mindful of your training; they are really no match for your anointing. God will let you know that the Pharaoh or the situation that stood in your way is removed or dead and the folks that would not accept you then, are crying out for help. The stage is now set, the scene is ready so go on and fulfill your call.

## ♦ Execution of Call

The final words for this situation are that there will be hindrances and there will be some that are not going to give heed to your voice. It might look like you are not fulfilling your calling, but keep going for the victory is going to be yours. Do not be dismayed, do not fear for by the time it's over God will destroy the powers of Egypt and you will find out that there is no God like Jehovah. Keep on doing what you are doing and after a while God will send the death angel.

If you have had traumatic experiences in your life and you stood diligently under the pressures of training, then you are destined to be triumphant. Regardless of the field of expertise that you specialize in your course shall never be the same; it shall be enlarged to frightening levels because of the discipline acquired during training. Society will notice, be attracted and they will call for you desperately to fulfill vacancies and bridge gaps. They will call for you to become the restorer of the breach. They will hand you so much power that you may have to pinch yourself to see if it is for real or you if you are dreaming because God's words must come to pass even in the midst of turmoil. He said that you shall prosper and be of good health; you shall be the head and not the tail; you shall be above only and not beneath. Whatever you put your hands to, it shall prosper because you suffered a little with God. So, you must now reign with him because the earth is His and He will give it in the hand of whom He will.

Therefore do not be afraid to apply when the positions open up for elected offices, the scriptures says, "When the righteous are in authority, the people rejoice: but when the wicked beareth rule, the people mourn" (Prov. 29:2). Who knows... if you were not brought to the kingdom for such a time as this!

Do not underestimate yourself either but reach for the challenges. If you see yourself as a grasshopper in the sight of the people, the people will see you as a grasshopper and if you see yourself as their deliverer they will see you as their champion. This is not the time to have drawbacks and fear, this is not the time to be ever learning and not being able to come to the knowledge of the truth. This is a time to step out in faith and conquer. If you can see it then you can have it, so practice to see yourself in the position, see yourself in the office with the big chair and the great view where the air condition is coolest in the building. You have to see yourself with the power to proclaim an executive order, and see yourself with the veto pen and with the final decision to defray evil. Whatever you do, see it to pass. It is imperative that you act and think like your Father (God) because you were made in His image and likeness. My mother used to say, the apple does not fall far from the tree; you are just like your daddy. Though she meant my physical father I will now apply it to mean my spiritual father and believe that she had indeed prophesied into my life.

Society will fall to their knees and beg for your presence. God will stir up the situation so hard that they will lose foolish pride and call frantically for your help. The same presence that they once despised they will now desperately call for, because the words must come to pass saying, "This is the stone which was set at nought of you builders, which is become the head of the corner" (Acts 4:11).

They will send for you from your solitary confines and places of lowliness because you are highly trained and qualified in the endeavor at hand and you have the spirit to analyze, interpret and determine directions.

There are too many magicians in secular places, they are working after their own ability, acting after their own council, thinking that they are the ones keeping the world spinning in its orbit and keeping the sun shining in its position but God is positioning a people to replace them on their assignment. What is about to hit this world they will not have the answer for and you are the appointed one for this time. You were brought to the kingdom for such a time as this so do not discount yourself and don't let any man despise your youth. I hope someone told Barack Obama that his age is not a disqualifier, all he has to do is allow the Spirit of God to speak to him and what they cannot solve, God will download into his spirit.

A generation is waiting on you therefore you have to act now. You are no longer in training so you must step up to the plate and deliver the true necessities that the glory of God may cover the earth. They are calling for you. The kings of the world are calling for you and you cannot go on your assignment with a rough look. You cannot go before the king in tattered clothing and the attitude of confines, so like Joseph, you have to shave and adorn yourself in the appropriate attire. You cannot go into the king's presence with signs that you have been in the prison of your dilemma. You cannot talk about how you were abused in the presence of the king's men, it is no longer about you, in fact it was never about you, this is bigger than self, therefore the pity parties will not work. The vision is for the nation and you are on assignment. Put the past behind, shave off the dead skin and put on a beautiful look regardless of your rough past. You have to take off the spirit of heaviness and put on the garment of praise. You have to go into the king's palace with praise in your mouth and a two-edged sword in your hand.

An entire generation is depending upon your wisdom and ingenuity to direct decisions. The history that God is now writing; this story that God is about to pen is not dependent on anyone else, but you. The entire history of Israel as a nation rested upon the shoulder of Joseph and you and I need to realize that this is our time and this is our season. A generation's survival and success is dependent upon our expertise. There are some people in your quadrant that will not make it if you don't understand that you are called by God. There are people that are dependent upon your voice, interpretation, understanding and your connection with God for their survival. God is going to use you to win a generation. This generation is not going to fail like the other generations. We are going to make a difference as we trust God to deliver us; as we do great exploits because we are loved and preferred by God, though we are going to be hated by others.

# 3 Triumph

*Now thanks be unto God, which always causeth us to triumph in Christ, and maketh manifest the savour of his knowledge by us in every place.*
*2 Cor. 2:14*

## ♦ Tools of Triumph

And he said, Thy name shall be called no more Jacob, but Israel: for as a prince hast thou power with God and with men, and hast prevailed (Gen. 32:28). Now that you are in the process of experiencing the triumphs that God distinctly said that you should have, like Jacob, you will have power with man and with God yet, you will face great resistance. However, it will be nothing that you cannot handle. When a person has tapped into their sacred call in their secular place, they have entered their designed destiny and the Lord will establish and settle that person. Triumph in this sense will not be measured only by affluence it is also measured by influence.

Every challenge will bring out a segment of your training. The most common resistance that you will come across will be in the form of jealousy. Even among your peers they will talk you into impotence if you allow them. It is not that people sit idle by and gossip about your victories or inabilities. You are in a position to effect change. Therefore, your words and actions are measured and weighed by everyone. For example, anything the President says, the media rips it apart, slices it at every possible angle and analyzes every possible meaning. You will experience similar scrutiny when you tap your destiny designed by God. You are the beacon that God appointed to give light and your words and action can have direct impact on the lives of the people within your sphere. Therefore careless words or actions will not be taken lightly.

You have to understand that you are in an envied position. All those who criticize could never wear your shoes nor take on your challenges much more to sustain it, but they can be a perfect mirror to highlight your deeds. At the same time you cannot allow them or any other people and what they talk about to stop you from experiencing the triumphs designed especially for you. People from time to time will talk negatively of the impression they receive and you cannot stop them. Neither should you be concerned about their views, as long you are in the 'right' because they cannot cancel out the destiny prepared for you. Therefore, let them talk all they want to talk. Don't be overly concerned with the critics, some things do not even deserve to be dignified with an answer. Because your mother, teachers, priest and God have already spoken into your spirit and you are convinced of your mission and mandate.

Therefore a simple brain floss and mind flush should keep you on track from the negatives that will follow your assignment. Hear and believe what God has declared because His words carry more weight than any other, and is final. It's amazing that they had nothing to say until God gave you the instructions. They always have the answer after the occasion. Don't be so concerned with the critics. Just remember, that it is not what is said, it is who said what.

I have no knowledge of God promoting a man without first training him. Therefore, your strength will reflect the course of your training and your giftedness will be in your hands.

This is the medium that was refined in the valley and you now have control over its power to dispense it at will with ease and versatility.

The giftedness being in your hands does not mean that it is between your fingers, it means the thing or ability endowed in your spirit by the Lord to do great exploits. Now for you to have total triumph you have to know that you have the tools for triumph. When Moses was between a rock and a hard place, in that, the Red Sea was before him and the Egyptians behind, the Lord asked him what's in your hands... hence you have to discover what is in your hands. What is it that you have authority over? Everything that you need is in your hands. When you release it and let it go, when you give it away then it will be transformed. When the Lord is through with it, it will blow your mind but do not lose your mind for it is going to go through some change but do not be frightened by what you see as it will not kill you.

Moses had a rod in his hands, he dropped it and it became a snake that scared him out of his wits. The little boy in the New Testament had five barley loaves and two little fishes which when he released them the Lord used them to feed over five thousand. Moses learned later how to use the rod, and when he stretched it over the Red Sea the waters were divided.

You have to know what is in your hand and how to administer it. Again the tools in your hands may have been a brother or sister or even a friend that was brought into ministry to help you do the Lord's work, but when you released them they are going through some negative changes and you cannot believe the transformation that has occurred. Before you release and partner with them into what God called you to do, they were loving and kind and did not bite, they did not have any venom in them but the change came and you were frightened. This means that you cannot put your trust totally in man; for the arms of flesh will fail you.

The Lord had twelve that were called to change the world. They were the tools in his hands, but one of them was a devil. Their behavior may be frightening but you have need for "that rod" so you will take it up by the tail and it will become what you want it to become again. Power has been endowed upon you and you shall triumph in your entire endeavor, but that does not take away from the fact that you must be as wise as a serpent and be harmless as a dove.

The enemy will not cease to come at you, but now you have power and the knowledge of how to use the power. You have to know when to attack and when to defend. Regardless of the direction or form that the enemy comes in, you must have the power to face up to and fight the enemy. You shall know that no evil shall come nigh your dwellings, neither shall any weapon that is formed against you prosper. God has the power to defeat the enemy that is trying to stop you from having your triumphant experiences and exposures. So, you have to release what is in your hand and let God transform it and teach you how to handle it.

Because the magicians are coming down the road, you have to know like Moses that your rod is not just a stick, but it is a serpent-eating stick. It is not just a piece of wood; it is something that can destroy the enemy; it can open the Red Sea. You have to discover the tool that is in your hand. You have been equipped to do battle and you will have to use what is in your hand.

Gideon in the Old Testament never needed thirty thousand men, he just needed three hundred to do the job, and God showed the world that it was not by strength nor by might but by His Spirit. All Gideon did was to obey the voice of the Lord, follow his instruction by selecting the men that lapped up the water like a dog...these were the men of valor. Therefore, you have to know the attack dogs that are assigned to you in the midst of your camp and position them strategically for warfare.

David was trained to take care of sheep; he had his practice of vigilance by killing a lion and a bear in defense of his flocks with the anointing in his hands. Later when the Philistine came to defy the armies of Israel he slew him with a sling and a stone (1 Sam. 17:49). Jephthah may be the son of a harlot but in the eyes of God he was a mighty man of valor and with a vow he brought the enemy down (Judg. 11: 1-30). Samson's dangerous appetite for delicate delights, caused him many hardships at the hand of his enemies, yet with the jawbone of an ass in his hand he killed a thousand Philistines (Judg. 15:15). Jael only had a simple glass of milk, a nail and a hammer in her hands and yet she destroyed the mighty captain of Sisera (Judg. 4:19-21). Jehoshaphat with just a song and a praise brought victory for Israel, and he did see the salvation of the Lord. These men and women, soldiers or deliverers used their gifts and tools to triumph and bring glory to God. "Because the foolishness of God is wiser than men; and the weakness of God is stronger than men" (1 Cor. 1:25). This type of experience and exposure will ultimately lead you into having triumphant experiences the world will talk about.

One of Barack Obama's obvious gifts and passion was that of a community organizer. He was ridiculed during the presidential primaries and general elections by his political opponents, as not having any executive experience; but he was not perturbed because it takes votes to win a election. So his perceived weakness became a weapon to defeat his opponents. He organized and mobilized communities village by village, town by town, county by county, and state by state. He did it in a manner never seen before in the history of our country. He used every medium available. To him every person was significant and every dollar valuable. In the end they all came out in great numbers and voted him in as the 44th President of the United States of America.

Take time to assess what is in your hand. God will always provide you with what you need to experience triumph. Whatever you need He has already provided!

Joseph was considered to be the overconfident younger son of Jacob. He was known to his older brothers as their father's favorite child. This idea was concretized in his older brothers' minds as they looked on to see their father bless Joseph with a specially made coat of many colors. For jealousy his older brothers conspired against him; sold him into slavery, and reported that he was mauled by animals. Joseph's present state did not destroy his divine destiny as he was confident that God would give him the strength he needed to endure.

Joseph's season of elevation finally came, now trained and gifts refined, God needed to set the stage and begin the process of promotion. Pharaoh became displeased with the service of his baker and butler and cast them into prison. This is a clear picture of what is happening today; some of the shifting we are seeing is due to an act of God, He is making positions for the promotion of His people. The reason why some folks are losing their jobs and the reason why the economy has fallen is all because God has to find a way to set up His people. If that is too deliberate to say let me rephrase and say it this way, everything is working for our good. We just need to let the process have its way. You might be lied on, sold out by others, wrongfully imprisoned and on top of all that be alive in a worldwide economic crisis. But decided to live because like you will see in Joseph's life, today might be a turning point for the fulfillment of the dream he gave you.

The knowledge of Joseph's ability to interpret dreams was not kept as a secret by the prison keeper. He told Pharaoh of Joseph's divine ability. Joseph was then sent for and called upon to interpret a dream that deeply distressed Pharaoh. None of Pharaoh's wise men whom were consulted had been able to make sense of the dream. However, Joseph accurately explained the symbols in the dream to a future time of abundance that would be followed by a time of great famine. Pharaoh was so impressed with Joseph's interpretation of his dream that he immediately rewarded Joseph with overseeing the land of Egypt.

This meant that Joseph was appointed leader of the Land. You may call him Prime Minster or President if you please. While the time was prosperous Joseph ensured that the abundance of the harvest was stored up for the time of famine to come. This was indeed great intellectual ability at work. Coincidentally during the years of famine, Joseph's brothers who obviously forgot about him came in search of grains and foods to keep their people from starvation. Joseph being a Godly man was very quick to forgive them and restore the breach.

### ♦ Taste of Triumph

Joseph's years of unwavering dependence and faith in God brought about not only the reunion of his beloved family but also his prestigious and high position of ruler of the land of Egypt. Due to this fact, Joseph was put in the position where he was able to save a nation from starvation and also brought about peace and resolution in his own family.

In today's society it is common opinion that it is impossible to keep a good man down. Joseph was one such man of his time. Despite the jealousy of his brothers and some misfortunes, Joseph was not defeated by his enemies; instead he triumphed in all his endeavours. Joseph was an astute believer in himself, his call and God. He had high self esteem and was very intelligent. He also possessed the ability to impress the right kind of people at the right time which lead to his ultimate triumph in his time.

We spent much time in the previous chapter illustrating and running a parallel with Joseph's life and ours by laying a foundational springboard of trauma to training and ultimately triumph because the pattern of his life from seventeen years old to the end had a sequential order that is applicable and relevant to all. However the true epitome of magnificence and triumph over trauma lies with the life of Moses, even though the scriptures did not lament much about his trauma but moved steadily towards his training and victories.

Joseph, unlike Moses was a dreamer that God cradled along from pit to prime minister with many variables in between. Moses, though guided by the Lord, actually grew up with kings and learned firsthand the intricacies of governing. He knew by the way of the Pharaohs how to engage the spirit of magicians and sorcerers from his youth.

Moses grew up in Pharaoh's house until he was a fully grown man. He saw how the law of the land permitted the maltreatment of the Israelites. This terrifying story caused Moses to become very distraught and concerned about the suffering of his own people under the hands of the Egyptians. At one point Moses witnessed one of his fellow Hebrew men being beaten by the Egyptians. He became so angry at seeing such injustice being done to a human being that he killed the offending Egyptian. Pharaoh found out about what Moses had done to the Egyptian and sought to have him punished by death. Moses, being aware of the plan to have him killed, ran away to a desert called Midian. He lived there with a priest for forty years until God called him to be deliverer of the Israelites from bondage and slavery (Exod. 2: 10-15). God had to take him totally out of the environment of Egypt to spend the equivalent time in the desert so he could be purged, lest at anytime in dire straits he resorted to his former mind-set.

Joseph did not do miracles instead he had the intellectual and spiritual ability to interpret and determine times and dreams but Moses was exposed from his childhood to a higher and more prestigious level of knowledge among the Pharaohs. Moses grew with all the skill of governing and probably was in line to become the next Pharaoh; he was a man of great stature and value in Egypt as he was the "son" of Pharaoh's daughter.

I strongly believe Moses was one promotion away from the throne. Hence it would seem easier in the eyes of man that God would just let him be king and change the course of the Israelites dilemma but God's ways are past finding out. This way Moses could not take any glory for himself. This way the world could observe and have a memorial to hold on to in dire times. This way they can say that if God did it back then he can do it again.

Moses' story is one of total triumph as he walked with God. His list of victories includes him living with a priest for forty years and being taught the protocols of the temple. Therefore, when he was challenged by a rival priest, he simply spoke to the earth and it opened and swallowed his opponents (Num. 16:30).

Moses showed dominance in the earth realm that has not been seen since Creation. God used Moses to demonstrate a magnificent show of his power in the display of the ten plagues.

All that Pharaoh tried did not work as God, through Moses, was more powerful than anything that Pharaoh's magicians tried.

The Bible records some high compliments that Moses received from God that no other person has ever received. The Bible recorded, "So the Lord spoke to Moses face to face, as a man speaks to his friend" (Exod. 33:11). The number one thing that God wants from each of us is an intimate personal relationship with him. Moses obviously accomplished all of this in his lifetime. After Moses had the direct encounter with God Himself, the Bible stated that he came back down off of the mountain with a face that shone so bright. The people were afraid to come near him due to the bright glow that was coming off his face after his being in the presence of the Lord. Moses then had to wear a veil over his face for a while so the glow would not overwhelm the rest of his people (Exod. 34:29).

Moses was so triumphant that when he held up his hand in battle Israel prevailed and when he lowered his hand they suffered defeat (Exod. 17:11). Though he had immense knowledge and great revelations he was also known as the meekest man of the planet that ever lived; in other words he defined the word humility. Yet he ruled with the presence and power of God. Moses traumatic experiences did not prevent him from becoming a great individual. His traumatic times pale into nothingness when compared to his triumphs. This leader was the essence of a royal priesthood and a holy nation.

In the New Testament era a thorn had to be placed into Paul's flesh to keep him in line because of the wealth of revelation that he had received but Moses in the Old Testament was too humble to need a thorn.

Strikingly though in his early years on the backside of the desert God was displeased with him because he did not circumcise his son on the eighth day according to the laws of the time. God sought a way to kill him though he was the pending deliverer but his wife Zipporah took a sharp stone, and cut off the foreskin of their child (Exod. 4:24-25).

People with a high calling have less of a margin for error because to whom much is given much is required and frankly, he had too much knowledge not to have known better. When you have so much invested power you have to be cognizant and cautious not to be overburdened nor stressed because the slightest of mistakes will bring severe consequences. That was Moses' pitfall when he struck the rock instead of speaking to it; he forfeited his opportunity to enter into the promise land.

Notwithstanding the man was so powerful in his lifetime that when he died God had to bury him personally; away from the presence of man and the devil. So protected by God, that the devil warred with Archangel Michael over the location of Moses' grave because he could not find it. Michael simply replied… "the Lord rebuke thee" (Jud. 1:9)! Yet that was not the end of Moses because in the transfiguration of Jesus Christ he was there and he will be back as one of the witnesses in the great tribulation.

Moses took what was for most an impossible mission and made it into reality with the help of God. The odds were totally against Moses accomplishing the great deliverance of the people of Israel. But God in his infinite mercy gave Moses the strength of character to accomplish a great job. Well done Moses.

Moses' story of triumph is a story for everyone to learn about. If anyone is faced with any situation which may appear to be impossible, remember Moses' story and what happened when he was willing to step out with enough belief and faith in God. Remember how he allowed God's power to operate and flow through him. Just remember that Moses changed the course of Jewish history with the deliverance of the Israelites from their slavery to the Egyptians. If God did this for the children of Israel through Moses, what will God not do for you today? After all God is the same God in Moses' time as is today.

Like the champions of old, be assured that everything that God has spoken to you is going to come to pass, regardless of your situation. It too shall pass when God gets you to where he promised because you are the ecclesia. You are the sacred of the almighty God, you are the friend of God. He deliberately placed you in the secular place where you are to transform the environment. He did not put you there to be at the bottom for the rest of your life; He intends to promote you; to cause you to become great; to be in charge and change the atmosphere into a Godly environment. You are assigned to be above and not beneath; the head and not the tail; every year there ought to be a gradual or radical promotion; you ought to be going from grace to grace.

There are many champions of our time that are extremely triumphant and glorify God with their legacy. People in both secular and spiritual circles have experienced trauma in their lives. But for some the best is yet to come or have come in the form of the triumphs they experience in their later years. Many can testify of the goodness of God in their lives as they experience many victories while others can speak of how they managed to get past their past and forge ahead with tremendous life changing experiences. Some of these experiences place them in positions they could only imagine and dream of; yet it became reality.

We examined the spiritual path of several great historical leaders who experienced triumph after their trauma and subsequent training, including Joseph and Moses. Jesus' life included trauma, training and the greatest triumph of all; He triumphed over the grave and the enemy of our souls. He is the ultimate victor; our Triumphant Lord and Savior.

We have discussed the traumatic experiences of Oprah Winfrey, Whoopi Goldberg, Maya Angelou, James Earl Jones and Barack Obama to name a few. Let us now look at the triumphant experiences of some of these personalities.

Oprah is considered to be one of America's most successful women. Her talent in show business and money making investments have made her one of America's wealthiest. Many Americans and people around the world see her as a role model and a great career practitioner to emulate. Oprah Winfrey in an interview in 1989 indicated that "It doesn't matter who you are, where you come from. The ability to triumph begins with you. Always" (American Academy of Achievement, 2009). This saying has much truth attached to it, as whatever we become in life solely resonates inside of all of us. Regardless of our background and conditions of early upbringing, we can soar like an eagle and excel with great accomplishment if we really want to.

Despite Maya Angelou's unfortunate upbringing and childhood trauma she became a seasoned poet and writer. Her talent and skills gave her recognition and some very good job offers. Maya also traveled extensively abroad. While away she studied many languages which she mastered, thus allowing her to communicate with a more diversified audience population. Maya Angelou became a national figure almost overnight and has become a big household name in America. She was nominated for a Pulitzer Prize. She has been invited by successive Presidents of the United States to serve in various capacities. President Ford appointed her to the American Revolution Bicentennial Commission and President Carter invited her to serve on the Presidential Commission for the International Year of the Woman. President Clinton requested that she compose a poem to read at his inauguration in 1993. Angelou's reading of her poem "On the Pulse of the Morning" was broadcast live around the world (American Academy of Achievement, 2009). So here you see misfortune should never be used as a stumbling block to prevent prosperity. Maya never allowed her mishaps to stand in the way of accomplishing her career goals and dreams to advance in society.

Another American achiever's name is written in history; she is Whoopi Goldberg. She has enjoyed tremendous success on television. She is a popular comedian. She won rave reviews hosting the annual Oscar telecast in 1994 and hosted the program again in 1996, 1999 and 2002. During the lifetime of her career she has won every major honor awarded by the entertainment industry. These awards run from the Oscar, Emmy, and Grammy to the TonyAwards. She has also received the Mark Twain Award for American Humor, presented in a 2001 ceremony at the Kennedy Center in Washington (American Academy of Achievement, 2009).

Notwithstanding, Whoopi had her share of childhood trauma, struggles with disappointments and setbacks. She however managed to get beyond the past and triumphed in the future. She has achieved so much for herself and others. After some personal struggles and the divorce from her husband she began to develop the character monologues that were to make her famous. After moving to the San Francisco Bay Area, she joined another improvisational group, the Blake Street Hawkeyes, and acquired a large local following for her work as a stand-up comedian. Soon she was touring the U.S. and Europe with her one-woman production, *The Spook Show* (American Academy of Achievement, 2009).

Yet another poet, and actor has conquered the odds to become a successful career personality. This person is none other than the great James Earl Jones "In 1968 Jones earned widespread acclaim for his performance in *The Great White Hope* playing a character based on Jack Johnson, the first African-American heavyweight champion." His sparkling performances in two plays won him two Tony Awards. He also received an Oscar nomination for his performance in the 1970 film version. James Earl Jones has received critical praise for his 1993 autobiography, *"Voices and Silences"* (American Academy of Achievements, 2009).

Sonia Sotomayor, the first Hispanic Justice and the third woman to serve on the US Supreme Court bench was nominated on May 26, 2009 by President Barack Obama. Sonia was able to rise to the top of the social and economic ladder despite socioeconomic hardships during her childhood upbringing. Her command of excellence from school days through university spoke to her great accomplishments even though she endured much hardship. Her achievements explain the reasons why it is not impossible for people to work against the odds to reach for the prize (Sotomayor Biography 2010).

Nelson Mandela never actualized until after he had spent years in prison. During his trials he never lost sight of his goal, trauma could not stop him and training never deterred from having the triumph of working with the people of South Africa. He was bigger than his prison. As soon as he was released from the walls of solitary confinement he picked up the pieces and carried on with his mission. Because of his determination to succeed he became the President of the African National Congress (ANC) and eventually the President of South Africa. Today Mandela's name is written in the history books.

Although Barack Obama had a roller coaster ride during his young life time he managed to ascend to the top of the political echelon, as he is today the 44$^{th}$ president of the great United States of America. His political career started shinning in 2004 when he was elected to the U.S. Senate as a Democrat, representing Illinois. It steadily gained momentum and blossomed after he gave a well-received keynote speech at the Democratic National Convention in Boston. In 2008 he ran for president as a Democrat and won by the largest margin of victory ever in the United States history to date. What a great sacred call to lead the people of one of the greatest secular places, the United States of America.

Despite all *trauma* experiences, if you stay the course and embrace your *training* you will enjoy the *triumph* of your **Sacred Call in Secular Places.**

# References

"American Academy of Achievement. James Earl Jones". January 14, 2009 <http://www.achievement.org/autodoc/page/jon2bio-1>.

"American Academy of Achievement. *Martha Stewart Biography*". January 14, 2009 <http://www.achievement.org/autodoc/page/ste0bio-1>.

"American Academy of Achievement. *Maya Angelou Biography*". January 14, 2009 <http://www.achievement.org/autodoc/page/ang0bio-1>.

"American Academy of Achievement. *Oprah Winfrey Biography*". January 14, 2009 <http://www.achievement.org/autodoc/page/win0bio-1>.

"American Academy of Achievement. *Whoopi Goldberg Biography*". January 14, 2009 <http://www.achievement.org/autodoc/page/gol0bio-1>.

Atherton, J. S. "Learning and Teaching: Piaget's". January 9, 2009
<http://www.learningandteaching.info/learning/piaget.htm.>.

"Biography of Barack Obama". January 14, 2009
<http://www.imdb.com/name/nm1682433/bio>.

Broude, Gwen J. Growing up: a cross-cultural encyclopedia.. California: ABC – CLIO Inc., 1995.

"The Caste System in Hinduism". August 23, 2010
<http://www.google.ca/search?sourceid=navclient&ie=UTF-8&rlz=1T4ADFA_enCA379CA380&q=The+Caste+System+in+India>.

Gauvain, Mary, and Michael Cole. (Ed.) Readings on the development. New York: W H. Freeman & Company, 1993.

Kaplan. Paul S, Adolescence. New York: Houghton Mifflin Company, 2004.

"The Life of Ronald Reagan: A Timeline". August 22, 2010
<http://www.npr.org/news/specials/obits/reagan/timeline.html>.

"Nelson Rolihlahla Mandela Biography". August 22, 2010
<http://africanhistory.about.com/od/mandelanelson/a/bio_mandela_3.htm>.

"Polygamy in Africa from a young Africans' point of view, 2010". January 23, 2010
<http://www.squidoo.com/polygamyinafrica>.

"Rastafari religion: rasta spirituality and religious beliefs". January 15, 2009
<http://www.important.ca/rastafari.html>.

Saisan, Joanna, Melinda Smith, and Jeanne Segal. "Child abuse and neglect recognizing and preventing child abuse". January 14, 2009
<http://www.helpguide.org/mental/child_abuse_physical_emotional_sexual_neglect.htm>.

"Socioeconomic status". North Central Regional Educational Laboratory. January 12, 2009
<http://www.ncrel.org/sdrs/areas/issues/students/earlycld/ea7lk5.htm>.

"Sonia Sotomayor Biography". August 22, 2010
<http://www.google.ca/search?sourceid=navclient&aq=2h&oq=&ie=UTF8&rlz=1T4ADFA_enCA379CA380&q=biography+of+sotomayer>.

Staszko, R. E. Today's early childhood educator: an introduction to the work and to the children (1st ed.). Canada: Darnley Publishing Group, 2004.

Uzgalis, W. "Stanford encyclopedia of philosophy". January 9, 2009
<http://plato.stanford.edu/entries/locke/>

"Socioeconomics". Wikipedia, the free encyclopedia. January 12, 2009
<http://en.wikipedia.org/wiki/Socio-economics>.

"What is child labor"? January 9, 2009
<http://www.childlaborphotoproject.org/childlabor.html#child>.

"Women in Rastafari". January 15, 2009
<http://www.islandmix.com/backchat/f27/women-rastafari-10308

CPSIA information can be obtained at www.ICGtesting.com
261124BV00002B/2/P